World Book's

SCIENCE & NATURE GUIDES

FOSSILS

OF THE WORLD

World Book, Inc.
a Scott Fetzer company
Chicago

Scientific names

In this book, after the common name of an organism (life form) is given, that organism's scientific name usually appears. Scientific names are put into a special type of lettering, called italic, *which looks like this.*

The first name in a scientific name is the genus. A genus consists of very similar groups, but the members of these different groups usually cannot breed with one another. The second name given is the species. Every known organism belongs to a particular species. Members of a species can breed with one another, and the young grow up to look very much like the parents.

An animal's scientific name is the same worldwide. This helps scientists and students to know which animal is being discussed, since the animal may have many different common names. Therefore, when you see a name like *Tyrannosaurus rex,* you know that the genus is *Tyrannosaurus* and the species is *rex* for this amazing dinosaur.

Fossil-collectors' Code

1 **Always go fossil hunting with a friend,** and always tell an adult where you are going.
2 **Don't damage the site** and don't take more than one specimen of each fossil— leave something for other collectors.
3 **Wear a hard hat** if you are exploring beneath a cliff. Check the cliff face carefully before you go near it, because loose rocks can fall on people.
4 **Ask permission before exploring** sites on private land.
5 **Leave fence gates as you find them.**
6 **Take your litter home.** Don't leave it to pollute the countryside.

This edition published in the United States of America by World Book, Inc., Chicago.

WORLD BOOK and the GLOBE DEVICE are registered trademarks or trademarks of World Book, Inc.

World Book, Inc.
233 North Michigan Avenue
Chicago, IL 60601 USA

For information about other World Book publications, visit our Web site **http://www.worldbook.com,** or call **1-800-WORLDBK (967-5325).** For information about sales to schools and libraries, call **1-800-975-3250 (United States); 1-800-837-5365 (Canada).**

Copyright © 2005 Chrysalis Children's Book Group, an imprint of Chrysalis Books Group Plc
The Chrysalis Building, Bramley Road, London, W10 6SP
www.chrysalis.com

Library of Congress Cataloging-in-Publication Data

Fossils of the world.
    p. cm. — (World Book's science & nature guides)
    "Edited text and captions based on A pocket guide to fossils by Chris Pellant"—T.p. verso.
    Includes bibliographical references and index.
    ISBN 0-7166-4212-3 — ISBN 0-7166-4208-5 (set)
    1. Fossils—Juvenile literature. I. Pellant, Chris. Pocket guide to fossils. II. World Book, Inc. III. Series.

QE714.5 .F587 2005
560—dc22
                                    2004043479

Edited text and captions based on *A Pocket Guide to Fossils* by Chris Pellant.

Illustrations by Mr. Gay Galsworthy; headbands by Antonia Phillips.

For World Book:
General Managing Editor: Paul A. Kobasa
Editorial: Shawn Brennan, Maureen Liebenson, Christine Sullivan
Research: Madolynn Cronk, Lynn Durbin, Cheryl Graham, Karen McCormack, Loranne Shields, Hilary Zawidowski
Librarian: Jon Fjortoft
Permissions: Janet Peterson
Graphics and Design: Sandra Dyrlund, Anne Fritzinger
Indexing: Aamir Burki, David Pofelski
Pre-press and Manufacturing: Carma Fazio, Steve Hueppchen, Jared Svoboda, Madelyn Underwood
Text Processing: Curley Hunter, Gwendolyn Johnson
Proofreading: Anne Dillon

Printed in China
1 2 3 4 5 6 7 8 9 10 09 08 07 06 05 04

Contents

Entries *like this*
indicate pages
featuring projects
you can do!

Introduction To Fossils

Fossils are what remain of plants and animals that lived from thousands to millions of years ago. They are a record of past life. A fossil can be made of the hard parts of a creature, like its shell or bone. It can also be formed from something that a creature made, like an egg, a footprint, or a burrow. Sometimes the entire creature is preserved—skin, fur, and all. Insects in amber or mammoths deep-frozen in ice are both examples of the latter phenomenon.

Classification of fossils

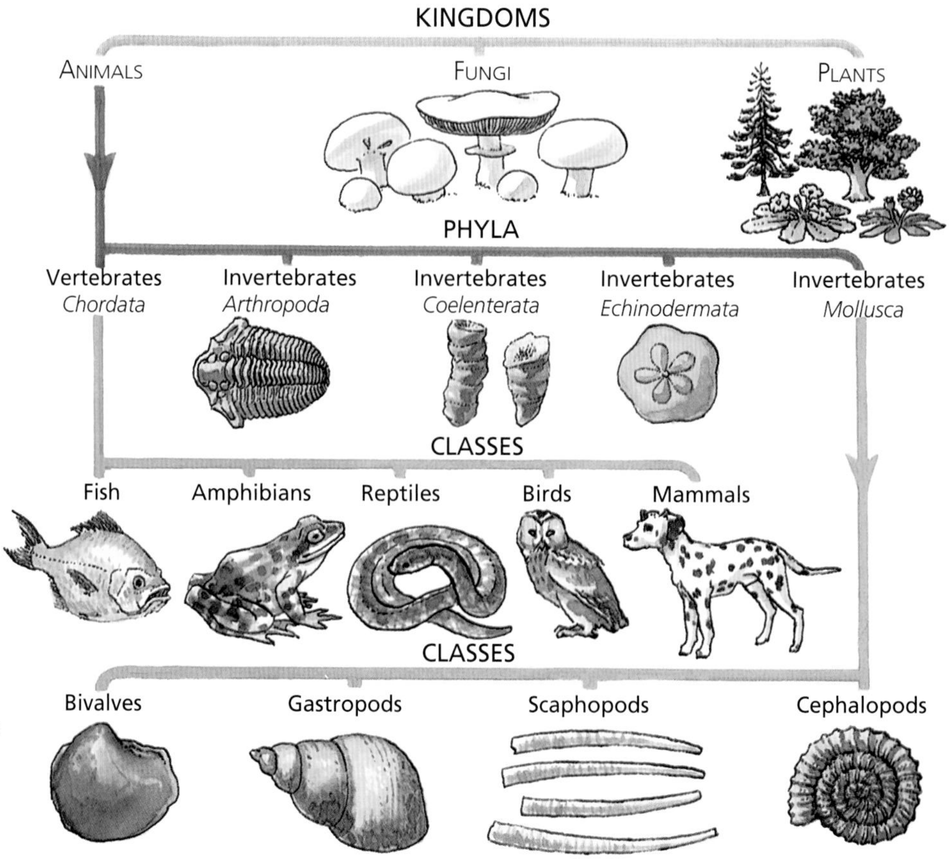

All living things—and all things that were once living—are called **organisms,** and they are classified by scientists into groups. The group into which an organism is placed is based upon the features it exhibits, its appearance, structure, behavior, and evolutionary history. Classification begins by sorting an organism into the largest general group, called a **kingdom.** (There are actually five kingdoms accepted by scientists. For the purposes of this discussion, the prokaryotes—one-celled organisms, such as the blue-green algae shown on page 15—and protists—one- or multi-celled organisms like true algaes and diatoms—are not included. Organisms from the remaining three kingdoms of fungi, plants, and animals are shown in the picture above right.)

Once a scientist determines to which kingdom an organism belongs, the organism is then placed within the smaller groups—such as **phyla, class,** and species. There are a large number of phyla and many classes, but only a few representative groups are shown in this picture.

KINGDOMS

ANIMALS — FUNGI — PLANTS

PHYLA

Vertebrates	Invertebrates	Invertebrates	Invertebrates	Invertebrates
Chordata	*Arthropoda*	*Coelenterata*	*Echinodermata*	*Mollusca*

CLASSES

Fish   Amphibians   Reptiles   Birds   Mammals

CLASSES

Bivalves   Gastropods   Scaphopods   Cephalopods

To classify a fossil, a scientist follows a series of steps (like those shown above) to determine into which categories a fossil best fits. For instance, if a fossil is determined to belong to the animal kingdom, the next determination to be made is whether the animal is a vertebrate (animal with a backbone) or invertebrate (animal without). At each classification step, the fossil is compared to other fossils and living things to help determine if it belongs to a new or an already existing species.

Breaking up and settling down

Weather breaks rock into small grains, called **sediments.** Rivers may carry these sediments to the sea. There, the sediments sink and are scattered over the seabed. New sediments are then scattered on top. Over time, the earlier and lower layers, or **strata,** are compressed and cemented together to form rock. Layers of sedimentary rock are being laid down all the time. They are forming now in rivers and seabeds. Bodies or pieces of dead creatures are falling upon these beds and being buried by new layers—these are the fossils of the future.

The wind, sun, and rain wear away the rocks.

Sediments are carried down to the sea by rivers and streams.

The sediments settle on the seabed in layers.

Pressure from the water above cements the sediments into hard rock.

How this book works

The opening pages of this book explain how sedimentary rocks are formed and how fossils are made. The book then gives examples of many different kinds of fossils. These examples are grouped together using the same methods that scientists use to classify organisms. The first section is about **plants,** and also briefly discusses blue-green algae and true algae. The second section is about **invertebrates.** The last section is about **vertebrates.**

Top-of-Page Picture Bands

Each group of organisms has a different picture band at the top of the page. These are shown below. They will help show you which section of the book you are in.

Plants

Sponges, Corals, & Echinoderms

Mollusks

Arthropods

Brachiopods

Vertebrates

Rocks On The Move

The surface of the earth is always in motion. Nothing stays the same for very long. Weather patterns change, rivers and glaciers follow new courses, mountains shift up, seas rise and fall. Some of these changes take place because the earth's rocks are moving.

Some sedimentary rocks are pushed down by the movement of the earth's crust to areas where temperatures are very high. There the rocks melt and may come to the surface again as molten rock (or **lava**). Other rocks are pushed up to form hills or mountains. Rocks can be twisted, or folded, or even turned upside-down. Then they may be exposed to the sun, wind, and rain. When rocks begin to break up and form sediment, this is the initial phase in the formation of sedimentary rocks, and so the cycle begins again.

The earth's crust is some 25 miles (40 km) thick, on average. It can be thicker underneath continents, but it averages only about 5 miles (8 km) thick beneath the oceans.

The outer core is about 1,400 miles (2,250 km) thick.

The mantle is about 1,800 miles (2,900 km) thick.

The inner core is about 1,600 miles (2,600 km) across.

Under our feet

The earth is actually made of layers. The top layer on which we live is the earth's **crust.** Below this is a thick layer called the **mantle.** Deeper still is the **outer core,** which is probably made of molten iron and nickel. In the center of the earth is the **inner core,** which scientists think is a solid ball of iron and nickel. The farther down into the earth you go, the hotter it gets. The temperature at the center of the earth is about 9000° Fahrenheit (5000° Celsius).

Floating plates

The crust and the upper part of the mantle are divided into some 30 sections called tectonic plates. These plates float and slowly move on the hot, flowing rocks underneath them. About 250 million years ago, the earth's land mass was one large continent. It broke up about 200 million years ago, and the continents that we know today started to drift away from each other. Their shapes and locations began to look similar to what they are today between about 70 and 30 million years ago. The continents move a few inches every year.

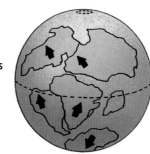

250 million years ago, there was just one large continent called Pangaea.

200 million years ago, Pangaea began to split into smaller continents.

65 million years ago, the continents had moved into the pattern seen in modern times.

Uplifting rocks

When these floating plates collide they sometimes push up rocks to make mountains, or rocks may be forced beneath plates at the edge of an ocean. Earthquakes often happen when plates rub against each other. Volcanoes are weaknesses along the boundaries between plates, where molten rock (**magma**) from below escapes to the surface as lava.

The movements of the land can cause sea levels to change. Deserts can become sea-beds and ocean floors can become mountain ranges. This is why fossils of sea-living creatures can be found on mountain tops.

Eventually, these drifting continents will meet once again to form one large land mass. Scientists believe this pattern has repeated two or three times in the last billion years. The continents have been moving since they started to form about 4 billion years ago. Scientists believe each pattern or cycle takes about 400 million years.

100 million years from now, the continents will have moved into a new pattern. The arrows show the direction In which the continents are moving.

Folding and faulting

Sedimentary rocks build up layer upon layer. When forming, the oldest layers are those lower down and the youngest are at the top. Unfortunately, the layers do not stay in this neat arrangement. As the land masses move, the layers buckle and fold. Faults form when this motion creates a fracture in the rock. As the rock on each side of the fracture moves and slips, the layers in the rock no longer align. This can make it difficult to match layers from two different areas, but it does push fossil-bearing rocks to the surface.

Exposed by erosion

Wind, water, and ice wear away rocks in a process called **erosion**. Sedimentary rocks are quite soft and are easily eroded. Water is a powerful force—rough seas can eat away at cliff faces, and rivers can carve deep valleys. Then the layers of sedimentary rock are exposed and so are the fossils within them. Fossil-bearing rocks are also exposed by the activities of people. When we dig quarries or cut through rocks to lay new roads, the layers in sedimentary rock may be exposed. The unwanted rubble left at a construction site may contain fossils. You should always get permission before collecting fossils in places like these, however.

How Do Fossils Form?

Many billions of living things have existed on the earth, but only a tiny number of them ever have (or ever will) become fossils. With some rare exceptions, fossils are found in sedimentary rocks. That's because the heat needed to form metamorphic or igneous rocks is so great it destroys any material that could become a fossil. Most of the sediments that formed sedimentary rocks were laid down in seabeds, and that's why most fossils found are from organisms that lived in the sea.

Turning to stone

There are several different ways in which fossils are formed. Many are turned to stone—that is, the substance of which the animal's shell or bone was made is slowly replaced by new minerals, like pyrite or quartz. This is called **petrification.**

Minerals are the natural components that make up the rocks of the earth. These minerals are washed into the fossil as they are carried through the surrounding rock by the liquids seeping through it. These liquids running through the rock can also dissolve or wash away the shell, leaving a hollow where the hard part of the animal once was. The hollow, or mold, is then filled in by different minerals. This is known as a **fossil cast.**

Organic sedimentary rock is made up mainly of fossils with just a little rock to hold them together. Shelly limestone is a term used to describe limestone that is rich in fossils. One small sample of this variety of rock may contain many different fossils.

Petrified fossil (turned to stone)

Tree cross section filled with opal

Shelly limestone

Fossils help to date rocks

Sedimentary rocks can buckle and fold because of pressures from beneath the earth's crust, but it is still possible to determine in which order they were laid down. Fossils can help us do this.

Some ancient organisms existed for only a short time, so their fossils appear only in certain layers. We can use the fossils to determine how old these layers are. Then, if we find a fossil of that organism again, in a different place, we can be certain of the age of the rocks in this second area. Fossils that help us do this are known as **zone** fossils.

Free-swimming, sea-living organisms make very good zone fossils. They used the oceans to spread to many different parts of the world. Their fossils help us to date and relate layers of rocks, which may be many hundreds or thousands of miles apart.

This ammonite *(Psiloceras planorbis)* is one of the zone fossils for the Jurassic Period

Insects in amber

Not all fossils are turned to stone. Insects, for instance, are sometimes preserved in amber—a hard, yellow-brown fossilized resin. Amber comes chiefly from the sticky resin of pine trees. Insects trapped and encased in resin are preserved in it. Under the right conditions, this resin can fossilize with the insect inside.

Clues to the past

Evolution is a theory describing the process by which plants and animals have changed over time to what they are now. These changes can sometimes allow the organism to be better suited to its environment, and thus more likely to reproduce and pass on its genetic traits. Fossils show us what changes groups of creatures have gone through.

Fossils can also tell us about ancient environments. We can compare fossil organisms to their relatives living today. For example, present-day corals live in warm, shallow seas. So it is likely that ancient corals (see pages 21-23) lived in the same kind of environment.

Plants

The earth was formed around 4.6 billion years ago. The earliest life found in fossil form dates to around 3.5 billion years ago. These were the cyanobacteria, sometimes known as blue-green algae. While not plants, these one-celled organisms used photosynthesis to convert carbon gases and the sun's energy into food—and then released oxygen as a by-product. Over time, cyanobacteria changed the composition of the earth's atmosphere to an oxygen-rich environment.

By about 1 billion years ago, one-celled plants—the earth's first plants—developed in the oceans. These plants also released oxygen as a result of photosynthesis.

Around 440 million years ago (mya) the first primitive plants appeared on land. During the Devonian Period (410-360 mya) the continents became covered in plants and forest. The plants were very small by our standards—the ceiling of the forest was only about 3 feet (0.9 meter) above the ground. During the Carboniferous Period (360-286 mya), the swampy, lowland areas of the continents were covered with very large ferns, and the first large trees appeared. Conifers and ginkgos dominated the forests about 150 mya and the first flowering plants appeared about 145 mya. Many modern types of plants developed during this time, known as the Cretaceous Period (145-65 mya). Because these plants were so like their modern relatives, scientists can discover how the climates (rainfall and long-term temperature) have changed in the last 65 million years. Much of what we know about how life on earth developed has come from studying fossils.

Plants

Alethopteris

These plants were seed ferns. Fossils of them are found as thin films of black carbon between layers of shale. The carbon is all that is left of the original plant. The leaves had a central stem with small leaflets along both sides.
Size: This specimen is 3¼ in (8 cm) long
Distribution: North America and Europe
Time range: Carboniferous

Cooksonia

These are important fossils. *Cooksonia* was one of the first plants to have vessels in its stem for carrying water and other fluids. At the end of the stems were spore cases that released spores into the air. New plants could grow from the spores, but only if the spores landed on moist ground. This is why this tiny plant lived in swampy places. It had no leaves, but it did have roots, which helped to secure it in the swampy ground.
Size: This specimen is 2¾ in (7 cm) across
Distribution: North America, Europe, Africa, Asia, and Antarctica
Time range: Silurian to Devonian

Calamites

These fossils are parts of plants called horsetails. They are a section of the stem. The center of the stem was once filled with soft tissue called pith. This pith rotted away quickly when the plant died, and the hollow stem then filled with sand. This fossil is a cast of that hollow stem. The markings running along its length are imprints of the vessels, which carried water along the stem. Fully grown plants were 65 feet (20 meters) high and shaped like pine trees.
Size: Section shown is 4¾ in (12 cm) long
Distribution: North America, Europe, and Asia
Time range: Carboniferous and Permian

Sphenopteris

Only the leaves of this plant are commonly found as fossils. Such fossils can be found in the form of a fern or a seed fern. It is thought that the plant lived in marshy places. The leaflets had slightly toothed edges.
Size: This specimen is 2½ in (6.5 cm) long
Distribution: Worldwide
Time range: Carboniferous to Permian

Lepidodendron

These fossils are actually part of a giant clubmoss. Many different kinds of clubmoss have been found, and these varieties once formed dense forests. The remains of these forests are preserved as coal. The fossil of a stem, shown here, has diamond-shaped markings on it where the leaves were once joined to the stem.

Size: Averaged 100 ft (30 m) tall, with a stem 39 in (1 m) across
Distribution: Europe, North Africa, North America, and Asia
Time range: Upper Carboniferous

Pecopteris

These seed ferns are commonly found as fossils. The plant had a woody stem and delicate leaves. Each leaf had a straight, central stem with egg-shaped leaflets along both sides. This specimen shows one leaf. It was found inside a lump of ironstone that formed within sedimentary rock.

Size: This specimen is 2½ in (6.5 cm) long
Distribution: Europe, North America, and Asia
Time range: Upper Carboniferous

Mariopteris

These plants were seed ferns. Today, all seed ferns are extinct, but they were common in the Carboniferous Period. Seed ferns had similarities both to ferns and to modern seed-bearing plants. The large leaves of Mariopteris were arranged in a spiral down the central stem. The leaflets of each leaf were narrow and had toothed edges.

Size: This specimen is 2¼ in (5.5 cm) long
Distribution: North America and Europe
Time range: Carboniferous

Plants

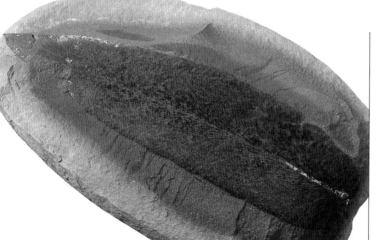

Neuropteris

This seed fern is usually preserved as a thin film of carbon between layers of sediment. Often the leaflets are no longer attached to the central stem of the leaf. This plant lived in swamps in which many layers of peat built up over time. This peat was later compressed and turned into coal.
Size: Leaves about 2 in (5 cm) long
Distribution: North America and Europe
Time range: Upper Carboniferous

Coniopteris

A thin layer of black carbon is often all that remains of the soft plant tissues of ferns. *Coniopteris* had a central stem with leaflets growing out at an angle. The leaflets were toothed on the upper edges.
Size: Leaves ¾ in (2 cm) long
Distribution: Northernmost North America, Asia, and Europe
Time range: Jurassic to Cretaceous

Williamsonia

This plant is related to the modern group of plants known as the cycads. Cycads are plants that look like thick-stemmed palms, and some types still survive today in tropical regions. They once formed forests with ginkgos and conifers. This fossil of *Williamsonia* shows the leaflets along either side of the leaf's central stem. It has been preserved as a thin, black layer of carbon.
Size: This specimen is 1¼ in (3 cm) long
Distribution: Worldwide—Time range: Jurassic

Acer

This group of trees can still be found today. It includes the maples. *Acer* is a flowering plant (angiosperm). The flowering plants did not develop until the end of the Jurassic Period, but they then developed very quickly and soon became the dominant plants on the earth. This fossil is of a leaf from an *Acer* tree. Such fossils are formed only where soft, fine sediments are laid down quickly.
Size: This specimen is 2½ in (6.5 cm) long
Distribution: Worldwide
Time range: Mid-Tertiary to Quaternary

Algae & Cyanobacteria

Not everything called algae is really a plant—or even algae! Important one-celled organisms, called blue-green algae, are not really algae at all. Blue-green algae, also called cyanobacteria, have a different cellular structure than other life forms—their cells contain no distinct nucleus. Dating back to some 3.5 billion years ago, cyanobacteria were among the first forms of life on the earth. Cyanobacteria belong to the kingdom Prokaryotae.

Ginkgo
Ginkgo biloba

This tree can still be seen today in many parks and gardens. It grows wild only in China. Fossils show that trees from the Ginkgo family have not changed for more than 150 million years, which is why gingko is known as a living fossil. There were once several species of ginkgos, but since the end of the Cretaceous Period about 65 million years ago, there has only been one. There are male and female ginkgo trees. Male pollen is formed on catkins. It is then blown by the wind to the female trees.
Size: Leaf is 1¼ in (3 cm) across, tree averages 60 to 80 ft (18 to 24 m) tall
Distribution: Once worldwide; now only native to China
Time range: Permian to Quaternary

Solenopora

Solenopora is truly an algae (a one-celled, photosynthetic organism with a distinct nucleus in its cell). *Solenopora* is a red algae, and the oldest algae fossils (at 1.9 billion years old) are from the red variety. True algae belong to the kingdom Protista.
Size: Area shown is 1½ in (4 cm) across
Distribution: Worldwide
Time range: Ordovician to Jurassic

Stromatolite

A stromatolite is not an organism. It is a type of deposit. Stromatolites are formed from the lime-rich material secreted by cyanobacteria; these deposits form in curved, layered mounds. The deposits are easily fossilized because the secretions are almost rock to begin with. The oldest of these fossils is some 3.5 billion years of age, but such mounds are still being formed by cyanobacteria today. Stromatolites vary in size but can be up to 20 inches (50 centimeters) high.
Size: This specimen is ¾ in (2 cm) across; the double mound is 4 in (10 cm) across—**Distribution:** Worldwide
Time range: Precambrian to Quaternary

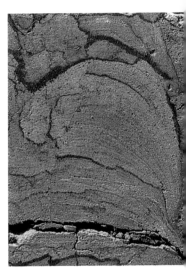

Looking for Fossils

You can look for fossils in your own area. Start by checking with the nearest state geological survey agency. The experts there should have listings or guides to significant fossil sites in your area and what they contain. You can also find out about an area's fossils by reading guide books, asking your local reference librarian to help you find useful information, visiting local museums, and checking on the World Wide Web.

If possible, always go on a field trip with someone who knows about fossils, like a teacher or an experienced collector. They can help you identify what you have found. You may want to join your local geological or fossil society.

Geological maps

A geological map may show you what age and type of rock is located at the surface in different areas (geology is the study of rocks, soils, mountains, volcanoes, rivers, oceans, other parts of the earth, and fossils). On some maps, contour lines show the height of the ground above sea level. You can use these lines to look for steep hillsides where the rocks have been eroded. These are good fossil-hunting places. Rivers, roads, and railroads, as well as other features of the land, may be shown as well.

It is a good idea to get to know what the different kinds of rocks look like. Sedimentary rock is the most important to the fossil hunter (see page 8). Limestone from the bottom of the sea, and shale from the mud laid down in the sea are the best rocks to look for.

Folds and faults

Sedimentary rocks are folded and twisted as the earth's crust moves. This pushes to the surface rocks that may otherwise have stayed deep inside the earth. These rocks need to be broken up and exposed before we can find the fossils within them.

This happens in several different ways: (1) A fault occurs when an area of the crust cracks and the two sides slide past each other. This may expose a cliff face of rock strata (layers). (2) Rocks are continually being exposed and worn away by the weather. Water is the main element at work here. (3) Rivers and streams carve valleys through the landscape; seas eat away at the land's edge. This results in steep-sided gullies and sea cliffs where the rock strata are exposed. As the rock is worn away, fossils that once were deep underground can be exposed. (4) People also expose rocks. Whenever we build new roads or buildings, we open up parts of the earth's surface.

These places are good for finding fossils, but never go on to sites like this alone or without getting permission in advance.

Extracting fossils

The best places to look for fossils is any place weathering is happening. Fresh fossils are being exposed in the layers all the time. There is no need to damage the rocks to reach them.

1 **Break off unwanted rock** if possible, so that the specimen is easier to carry home. Always wear protective eye gear.

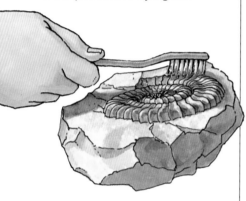

2 **Some fossils only need to be brushed clean.** Others need to be scraped to remove unwanted sediments. Be careful that your tools do not damage the fossil. Work gently so as not to break the specimen.

3 **Paint the specimen with varnish** to protect it.

What you need

1 **Footwear:** walking boots are best, but strong high-top sneakers laced up properly will protect your feet and ankles against loose or sharp rocks.
2 **Clothes:** in hot weather make sure you have light clothes that will also protect you from sunburn. If it is likely to rain or be cold, wear waterproof or warm clothes. Listen to the weather forecasts.
3 **Gloves:** you need a strong pair to protect your hands from sharp rock fragments.
4 **Hard hat or other protective head gear:** wear a hard hat if you are below cliffs or places where there may be falling rock.
5 **Lightweight backpack:** this is the most comfortable way to carry your equipment and finds, and it leaves your hands free.
6 **Field notebook with pencils and pens:** make notes about a fossil find—include the date, the weather, location, and the rock type your fossil came from, so that later you can write up an entry in a fossil diary.
7 **Hand lens:** buy one that is 10 power (labeled x10), and wear it on a cord around your neck. A rock store or museum shop will have one.
8 **Trowel:** for digging specimens out of earth. But don't use it to pry fossils out of the rock because you may damage them. You can find loose specimens very easily on most sites.
9 **Camera:** if you take photographs of fossils, rather than prying them out, it avoids damaging the environment.
10 **Bags and containers:** take strong cloth bags for large specimens. Small, self-sealing, plastic bags are good for small specimens. Newspaper and bubble wrap are useful for protecting delicate fossils.
11 **Small notepad or a roll of self-adhesive labels:** they are easier to use for notes about your specimens than trying to write on the bag itself.

Invertebrates

Invertebrate is a general name that describes a huge range of animals with no internal backbones. Some invertebrates, like worms or jellyfish, have no backbone at all. Others, like mollusks, insects, and lobsters, have exoskeletons (hard cases or shells on the outside of their bodies).

The oldest known invertebrate fossils date from about 700 million years ago (mya). These wormlike and jellyfishlike animals descended from more primitive (basic) animals. These invertebrates very rarely formed fossils.

It was not until invertebrates began forming shells at the start of the Cambrian Period (544-505 mya) that many fossils appear.

All the groups of invertebrates featured in this book evolved between 544 and 248 mya (the end of the Permian Period). Most of these animals lived in the sea and many grew to enormous sizes. As plants colonized the land during the Devonian Period (410-360 mya), invertebrates that were able to live on dry land evolved. Huge dragonflies hunted in the swamps of the Carboniferous Period. By the time the first vertebrates ventured on to dry land, there were plenty of invertebrates for them to eat.

Invertebrates continued to evolve during the Jurassic and Cretaceous periods. In the seas, the mollusks evolved to take many different forms. A most successful group was the ammonoids, with thousands of species. They died out around 65 mya in the event that caused large numbers of species to become extinct at the end of the Cretaceous Period.

Sponges & Corals

Sponges, Corals, & Echinoderms

Sponges live today in both salt and fresh water. They have a baglike structure with an opening on the upper surface, and may have a long stalk on the bottom surface.

Water goes into the sponge through many small openings all over its body. The creature takes food and oxygen from this water. The water leaves the sponge through the larger top opening. The skeleton of most sponges is made up of hard spiky structures called "spicules." These are well preserved as fossils.

Thamnospongia

These fossils are shaped like a crooked root. Their outer surface is rough and covered with tiny holes, or pores. This specimen was found inside a lump of flint—a hard stone made of quartz crystals that breaks with dangerously sharp edges. These crystals may have been formed from the skeletons of sponges that died millions of years ago.
Size: This specimen is 3¼ in (8 cm) across
Distribution: Worldwide—Time range: Cretaceous

Siphonia

These tulip-shaped sponges were fixed to the seabed by a stalk with rootlike appendages. These appendages are not usually preserved in fossil form. The rounded part of the sponge had many small pores, which led to canals inside the organism. These joined a large canal that reached from the upper surface to the center of the sponge. The small canals brought water into the sponge and the larger one removed it.
Size:
This specimen is
1¼ in (3 cm) long
Distribution: Europe
Time range:
Cretaceous to Tertiary

Ventriculites

Sponges belonging to this genus were shaped like narrow vases. Some of the fossilized forms of this sponge can be found complete with roots. The walls of the sponge were thin, with grooves running up and down and from side to side over the surface. The skeleton of spicules had six branches. Present-day relatives of *Ventriculites* live in warm European seas.
Size:
This specimen is
1¼ in (3 cm) long
Distribution: Europe
Time range:
Cretaceous

Corals are a group of small, soft-bodied animals. The individual cylinder-shaped coral creatures are called polyps. Most coral polyps live in colonies, with each polyp inhabiting a tube-shaped cavity. In most types of coral, each polyp forms an external skeleton, or wall, made of calcium carbonate (limestone) around its cavity. These small, walled cavities are called corallites.

The inside of the corallite may be divided into chambers by sheets of material, called tabulae. There may also be internal walls running from top to bottom called the septa, which grow outward from the center to the outside walls. From above, the septa form a pattern like the spokes of a bicycle wheel.

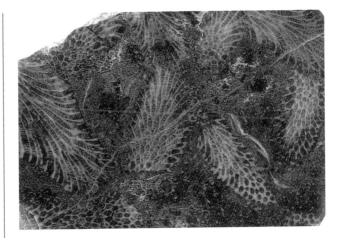

Thamnopora

Thamnopora grew outward in many branches to about 14 inches (35 centimeters) across. It is now extinct. The photograph shows a specimen which has been cut crosswise and polished. The tabulae show up as thin, pale lines within each corallite.
Size: Area shown is 3¼ in (8 cm) across
Distribution: Worldwide—Time range: Devonian

Favosites

These coral animals lived in colonies made up of many small, closely packed corallites. The outline of the colony was rounded. From above you can see that the corallites have several straight sides. This is called polygonal cross section. It makes the colony look like a piece of honeycomb. *Favosites* once lived in shallow seas but is now extinct.
Size: This specimen is 3½ in (9 cm) across
Distribution: Worldwide
Time range: Upper Ordovician to Middle Devonian

Dibunophyllum

These corals lived alone and not in a colony; they could grow up to 1½ inches (4 centimeters) across. The genus is now extinct. This specimen has been cut crosswise so that the septa can be seen as lines going into the center from the outer edge. Only some of the septa reach into the center of the coral. The outside walls of *Dibunophyllum* were thickened by weblike masses of calcium carbonate called dissepiments.
Size: This specimen is ¾ in (2 cm) across
Distribution: North America, Asia, Europe, and North Africa
Time range: Lower Carboniferous

Corals

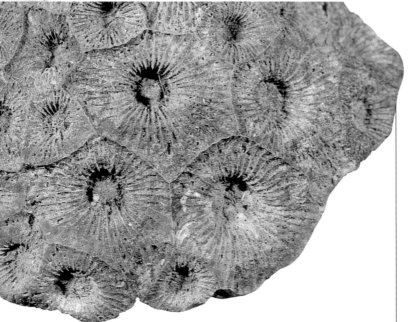

Thysanophyllum

This coral lived in colonies. Each corallite was packed closely to its neighbors. They had angular outlines of six or eight sides. The septa reached to nearly the middle of the corallites. The outside walls were thickened by dissepiments.
Size: This specimen is 4 in (10 cm) across
Distribution: Europe—Time range: Carboniferous

Lithostrotion

This coral formed a colony which looks like a mass of roots when fossilized. There were tabulae and septa. These fossils are common in limestone rocks and calcite-containing shales (a type of rock that splits easily into fine layers). It is also called *Lithostrotionella* or *Acrocyathus*.
Size: This specimen is 2¾ in (7 cm) across
Distribution: Europe, North America, North Africa, and Australia
Time range: Carboniferous

Cyathophyllum

These corals lived alone. They varied in shape from long and thin to cone-shaped. The septa stretched from near the center of the coral to its outside walls. They can be seen as thin lines on the long, thin specimen in the photograph. The hollow on the top of the coral was very shallow.
Distribution: North America, Europe, Asia, and Australia
Time range: Devonian

Ketophyllum

This coral animal lived alone. The photo below shows the deeply ridged outside of this cone-shaped coral, and the photo to the right shows the inside of the same specimen. The hollow in the top of the corallite was deep. The septa did not reach the middle. *Ketophyllum* was fixed to the seabed with rootlike structures, which are sometimes preserved.
Size:
This specimen is 3¼ in (8 cm) long
Distribution: Europe and China
Time range: Silurian

Lonsdaleia

This extinct coral lived in colonies. There was a deep dip on the top of each corallite where the polyp lived. There was also a central column running from top to bottom of the organism. The septa reached up to the central column.

Size: Each corallite is about ⅓ in (0.8 cm) across
Distribution: North America, Europe, Asia
North Africa, and Australia
Time range: Carboniferous

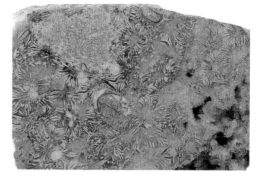

Thamnastrea

This specimen has been cut crosswise. The corallite walls of this organism were not well formed and seem to join with each other. This coral often formed large masses, which branched outward. *Thamnastrea* built reefs with other corals such as *Isastraea*—these coral-reef masses could reach more than 4 feet (1¼ meters) across. This coral is often preserved in oolitic limestone (limestone formed in small, round grains).

Size: The area shown is 2 in (5 cm) across
Distribution: North and South America, Europe,
and Asia
Time range: Triassic to Cretaceous

Thecosmilia

This coral lived in warm, shallow seas and was a reef builder. The septa of *Thecosmilia* were straight walls of calcite that spread out like rays from the center in groups of six. The outside walls of each corallite were made stronger by dissepiments. It is often fossilized in oolitic limestones (limestone formed in small, round grains).

Size: The single,
whole specimen is
1¼ in (3 cm) wide
Distribution:
Worldwide
Time range: Triassic
to Cretaceous

Isastraea

The six-sided corallites of *Isastraea* were closely packed in large colonies. The septa grew in groups of six. Some of the septa were long and extended from the edge to the center of the coral. The colony itself was a rough tube-shape, narrower at the bottom than the top. This was a reef-building coral.

Size: The specimen
is 2½ in (6.5 cm) long
Distribution:
Europe, North
America, and Africa
Time range:
Jurassic to
Cretaceous

Sea Urchins

Sponges, Corals, & Echinoderms

The soft body of a sea urchin, a type of echinoderm, is safely protected inside its shell, or "test." This test can vary considerably in shape, from round to oval or heart-shaped.

The test is made of bands of two types of plates, which usually run from top to bottom around the animal. The narrow bands—ambulacra—are made of plates that have pores. The broader bands running between the ambulacra are called the interambulacra. In living species, delicate tube-feet—used for moving, and sometimes also for feeding and breathing—pass through the pores.

"Regular" sea urchins have a test that appears to be divided into five segments. Their mouth is always centered underneath the body and the anus (waste-expelling hole) is on top. "Irregular" sea urchins may have their mouth and anus in varying parts of the shell, and their ambulacra vary in shape. Many sea urchins have masses of spines covering the test, but these often break off before the fossil forms. Sea urchins are common inhabitants of modern oceans.

Holectypus

This sea urchin had a round test, which looked slightly domed when seen from one side. The underside, where the mouth was, was flat or slightly hollowed and had several large swellings. Holectypus was an irregular urchin; the anus was on the side. Its ambulacra were fairly straight, reaching around from the upper to the lower surface.

Size: This specimen is ¾ in (2 cm) across
Distribution: Europe, North America, North Africa, and Asia
Time range: Lower Jurassic to Upper Cretaceous

Cidaris

This specimen has been preserved with its spines, which makes it an unusual fossil. Usually the spines are broken away from the test during the fossilization process, and are thus preserved separately. This is a regular sea urchin—the mouth and anus are in the center of the lower and upper surfaces respectively.

Size: This specimen is 1¼ in (3 cm) across
Distribution: Worldwide
Time range: Triassic to Quaternary

Cassiduloids

These are a group of small, irregular sea urchins. The outline of the test is almost round, but it looks as though it has five sides. The ambulacra are petal-shaped and do not reach all the way around the test. They form a star shape on the upper surface. The anus can be seen at the edge of the right side of the specimen.

Size: This specimen is 1½ in (4 cm) across
Distribution: Worldwide
Time range: Tertiary to Quaternary

Holaster

This sea urchin was irregular. The test was somewhat heart-shaped, with a slightly domed upper surface and a slight point at the rear end. The ambulacra were petal-shaped and had slit-shaped pores arranged in pairs. The interambulacra were broad. There were small swellings on the upper surface and larger ones below.
Size: This specimen is 3½ in (9 cm) across
Distribution: Worldwide
Time range: Lower Cretaceous
to Upper Tertiary

Size: Up to 1½ in
(4 cm) across
Distribution:
North America,
especially California
Time range: Tertiary
to Quaternary

Dendraster

This is a common genus of irregular sea urchins. Often they form a large part of the rock in which they are found. The fossils are oval in outline and very flat. *Dendraster* is commonly known as a "sand dollar." Its ambulacra are petal-shaped and do not reach all the way around the test; they begin at a point at the rear end of the upper surface. The anus is on the outside edge of the lower surface and has a groove above it.

Echinocorys

This irregular sea urchin had a domed upper surface and a flat base. The ambulacra were quite straight and had their pores arranged in pairs. A ridge ran across the test between the mouth near the front and the anus at the pointed back end of the animal's underside. The wide interambulacra had small swellings. *Echinocorys* may have lived partially buried in the seabed.
Size: This specimen is 3¼ in (8 cm) across
Distribution: North America, Europe, and Asia
Time range: Upper Cretaceous

Sea Lilies & Starfish

Sponges, Corals, & Echinoderms

Sea lilies are a type of echinoderm that look like plants, but they are really animals. They have a stalk and a flowerlike structure called a calyx (plural: calices)—in which the animal's delicate body may be found. Arms grow out from the calyx; these arms may be branched with finer branches called pinnules. These pinnules create a sort of net for collecting food, which is then wafted into the mouth in the center of the calyx. The stem is made of calcite plates called ossicles, which vary in shape. The calyx is made of larger plates.

Clematocrinus

This was a genus of small sea lilies. This specimen shows the calyx and arms with many slender branches. Only fragments of the stem were preserved.

Size: This specimen is 1 in (2.5 cm) long
Distribution: North America, Europe, and Australia
Time range: Middle Silurian

Macrocrinus

This specimen features two calices, one with a length of stem. Pinnules would have formed a feathery funnel around the mouth, which was deep in the center of the small calyx. There were hairlike cilia on the pinnules, which would have wafted food toward the mouth. The ossicles on the stem became larger as they got farther away from the calyx.

Size: The larger specimen is 1½ in (4 cm) long
Distribution: North America
Time range: Lower Cretaceous

Metopaster

This strange creature was a starfish. It was related to the sea urchins and sea lilies. It had a five-sided outer wall of large plates that formed the shape of a five-pointed star, with many smaller plates within.

Size: Members of this genus grew to a maximum of 2½ in (6.5 cm) across
Distribution: Europe
Time range: Cretaceous to Tertiary

Encrinus

This sea lily had a small calyx and well-developed arms. There were 10 arms with many pinnules. The zigzag connections between the plates on the arms can be seen clearly. *Encrinus* lived in shallow, flowing seawater with its calyx facing the current. The densely packed pinnules sifted food from the water.
Size: This specimen is 1½ in (4 cm) long
Distribution: Europe, except for Great Britain
Time range: Middle and Upper Triassic

Scyphocrinites

This specimen shows the calyx and branched arms of a sea lily that grew to over 40 inches (100 centimeters) long. The calyx was made of different kinds of plates—large ones at the base where the calyx joined the stem and smaller plates on the upper portion of the calyx. At the base of the stem was a bulbous structure where the animal was held to the seabed.
Size: Area shown is 4 in (10 cm) long
Distribution: North America, North Africa, Asia, and Europe
Time range: Upper Silurian to Devonian

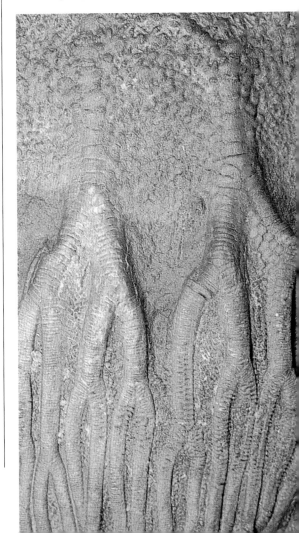

Palaeocoma

This is a genus of brittle stars. *Palaeocoma* had a central disk made of many small plates and long snakelike arms. It is closely related to present-day brittle stars. When conditions were right, large numbers of these creatures were fossilized.
Size: Central disk up to ¾ in (2 cm) across
Distribution: Europe—Time range: Jurassic

Pentacrinites

The stem of this genus of sea lilies could be over 40 inches (100 centimeters) long. The stem ossicles were star-shaped. The small calyx had long arms with pinnules. Single fossils of *Pentacrinites* are often found in shales and limestones. Closely related modern species sometimes leave the seabed and swim freely.
Size: Area shown is ¾ in (2 cm) long
Distribution: North America and Europe
Time range: Triassic to Tertiary

How Fossils Got There

Fossils are found between layers, or strata, of sedimentary rock. These strata are being laid down all the time—in the present, as well as for much of the earth's history. The strata range from a fraction of an inch to several feet thick. Forces beneath the earth's crust can fold and twist the layers, which can make it difficult to work out the order in which the layers were laid down. This action also pushes fossils to the surface that would have remained buried.

Find out about strata

You will need: several lengths of modeling clay in different colors, some shells, and a butter knife.

1 **Roll out the lengths of clay** into strips that are long, flat, and about 1 inch (2.5 centimeters) wide. Make them different thicknesses.
2 **Place a shell on the "seabed"** on each layer before laying down another strip. The shells are your "fossils."

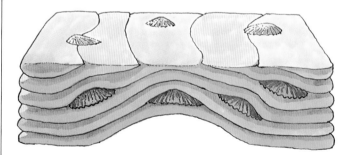

3 **Lay one strip on top of another.** The first strip represents the seabed. Each strip placed on top will be a new layer of sediment laid down.
4 **Complete all the layers.** This is how an undisturbed section of sedimentary rock would look. The youngest layers are at the top.

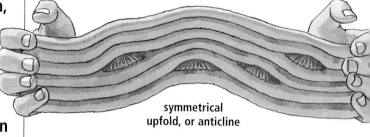

symmetrical upfold, or anticline

5 **Push the ends of your model together.** This represents the movement of the earth's crust.
6 **If you push equally hard at each end,** the strata will form a symmetrical upfold, or anticline. A symmetrical downfold, or syncline, may also occur.

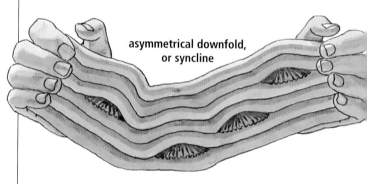

asymmetrical downfold, or syncline

7 **If you push harder at one end** than the other, an asymmetrical upfold or downfold may occur.

8 **Cut off the top of an anticline** with the knife. The knife represents weathering of the seabed after the sea has receded or moved.
9 **You can see that all the layers,** even some of the oldest, may be exposed. Fossils can be at or just below the surface.

Make your own fossil

You will need: Plasticine (playdough won't work), plaster of Paris, self-hardening modeling clay and a plastic container.

1 **Make a fossil shape** out of the plasticine.
2 **Find an old plastic container** that is deep enough to hold your "fossil."

3 **Mix up enough plaster of Paris** to fill the container halfway, and pour it in. Before it sets, press your "fossil" into the plaster.

4 **Roll out some plasticine** into thin lengths. Use them to cover the surface of the plaster. Go right up to the edges of the container and mold them around the "fossil."

5 **Mix some more plaster of Paris** and pour it over the thin plasticine layer. Make sure that it covers your plasticine-topped "fossil," and let it set.

6 **When the plaster is hard,** take it out of the container, separate the two halves, and peel away the plasticine. Remove the fossil shape. The two halves of the solid plaster now form a mold.

7 **Dust the inside of both halves** of the mold with talcum powder (but don't breathe it in).

8 **Press a soft lump of self-hardening modeling clay** into one half of the mold. Firmly press the other half of the mold on top.

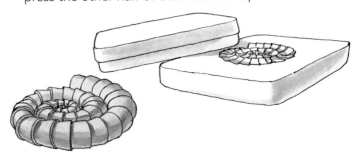

9 **Open the two halves of the mold.** Inside will be a "fossil" cast (see page 8) of your original model. The modeling clay represents the minerals that replaced the material from which the original shell was made.

Bivalves

Mollusks

There are many different kinds of mollusks. Most of them have a shell protecting the outside of their soft bodies. Beneath the shell is a slippery skinlike organ called the mantle. The shape of the shell varies, depending on where and how the mollusk lives.

Bivalves are a kind of mollusk. They live in oceans, lakes, and ponds. Some are fixed to the bottom, others burrow, some can swim, and others move along the seabed with the aid of a fleshy foot that pokes out of the shell. The shell is in two often identical parts, called valves. These are hinged and can be opened and closed by the animal's muscles. The pointed end of the shell is the front and is called the umbo (plural: umbones.) Two siphons, or tubes, also exit from the shell. One siphon sucks food into the mouth, while the other removes waste. Bivalves are common fossils.

Dunbarella

These semicircular bivalves had very pointed umbones. The hinge line was straight and there were winglike flaps on either side of the umbones. The thin valves were marked by ribs spreading out from the umbo and faint growth lines.
Size: Up to 1½ in (4 cm) across
Distribution: North America and Europe
Time range: Carboniferous

Schizodus

This genus of oval-shaped bivalves had very faint ribs and growth lines. Its umbones stuck out. This specimen is a cast fossil—the original shell dissolved away, leaving a hollow space (see page 8.) The fossil is made of sediment that filled up the empty space. *Schizodus* lived on the slopes of reefs in deep water. It is found with sea lilies, brachiopods, corals, and trilobites.
Size: Up to 2 in (5 cm) long
Distribution: Worldwide
Time range: Carboniferous to Permian

Nuculana

These small bivalves with a triangular outline have umbones that are at the front and the shell is elongated toward the rear. Growth lines can be seen. Today, *Nuculana* still exists. It burrows into the seabed and pokes siphons through to the surface. These bring food and oxygen into the shell and release waste back into the water.
Size: Up to ¾ in (2 cm) long
Distribution: Worldwide
Time range: Triassic to Quaternary

Carbonicola

This group of bivalves lived in lakes and rivers at the time of the great Carboniferous forests—these forests later formed coal deposits. *Carbonicola* umbones faced forward, while the valves were shaped like a broad triangle. There are lines on the shell that show the stages of growth. *Carbonicola* probably used a fleshy foot to move through the mud.

Size: Up to 2.5 in (6.5 cm) long
Distribution: Europe
Time range: Upper Carboniferous

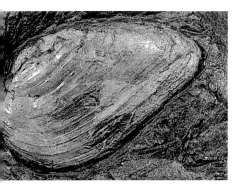

Oxytoma

These almost round bivalves had one valve that curved outward more than the other. There were wings on each side of the umbones. Some varieties also had a large spine growing out from the umbones. The valves had several thick ribs, and the shell was sometimes extended where those ribs reached the outer edge. There were finer ribs between the thick ones and faint growth lines.

Size: About 1¼ in (3 cm) long
Distribution: Worldwide
Time range: Upper Triassic to Upper Cretaceous

Anthraconauta

This photograph shows a large number of *Anthraconauta* preserved in shale. The thin shell was elongated and there were clear growth lines. These bivalves lived in streams and rivers surrounded by vast Carboniferous forests.

Size: Up to 2 in (5 cm) long
Distribution: Europe
Time range: Carboniferous to Permian

Cardinia

The outline of these bivalves was oval or triangular and the shell had thick growth lines. The valves were thick and strong, which enabled the bivalve to survive being jostled and jolted in shallow seas. *Cardinia* is found in sandstones, shales, and mudstones with ammonites, other bivalves, gastropods, and belemnites.

Size: Average ⅝ in (1.6 cm) long
Distribution: Worldwide
Time range: Upper Triassic to Lower Jurassic

Bivalves

Mollusks

Chlamys

The valves of *Chlamys* were not exactly identical—one was more domed than the other. The shell had round outer edges, but was straight at the hinge. The spines on the valves of this specimen apparently broke off before fossilization. There are large earlike growths on the valves. Some species of this genus were fixed to the seabed by a mass of threads, called a byssus, while others swam.

Size: Up to 4 in (10 cm) long—Distribution: Worldwide
Time range: Triassic to Quaternary

Lopha

A genus of thick-ribbed oysters, *Lopha* has strong valves that allow it to survive on a bed of choppy, shallow seas. The valves meet at a zigzag edge. The valves of this specimen have been separated. The inner surface (on the right) has a scar where a muscle was attached.

Size: Up to 4 in (10 cm) long
Distribution: Worldwide
Time range: Triassic to Quarternary

Exogyra

Oysters have two valves very different in form from one another. One valve is flat, while the other curves outward. In the oyster genus of *Exogyra*, the shell was a spiral shape with the umbones coiled toward the rear end. The outline of the outer edge was round, and the valve edges were toothed or notched. There was also a deep ridge on the shell. *Exogyra* lived firmly attached to the seabed.

Size: Up to 8 in (20 cm) long
Distribution: Worldwide
Time range: Cretaceous

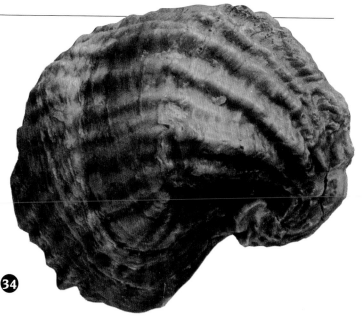

Plagistoma

These bivalves had a shell marked faintly by growth lines. Their outline was slightly triangular, although the edge of the rear end was rounded. At the front end, near the umbones, was a small wing-shaped piece. Both valves curved outward and were the same size. *Plagistoma* lived on or just below the seabed, sometimes attached by a byssus.

Size: Up to 4¾ in (12 cm) across
Distribution: Worldwide
Time range: Triassic to Cretaceous

Myophorella

This bivalve had thick, curved valves and inward-pointing umbones. The valves had widely spaced rows of bumps that look like lengths of heavy rope where fossilized. Each valve had one straight and one curved edge. This bivalve lived in shallow waters, burrowing a little way into the seabed.

Size: Up to 4 in (10 cm) long
Distribution: Worldwide
Time range: Jurassic to Cretaceous

Camptonectes

A large bivalve with a rounded shell but a straight line at the hinge, the shell had clear growth lines and came to a point at the umbones. These umbones had wings on each side. *Camptonectes* was attached to the seabed (or other objects) by byssal threads. Specimens are found in sandstones and mudstones with other fossil bivalves, sea urchins, and brachiopods.

Size: Grew up to 8 in (20 cm) across
Distribution: Worldwide
Time range: Lower Jurassic to Upper Cretaceous

Bivalves

Mollusks

Inoceramus

Broad ridges ran across the valves of these bivalve mollusks. The overall shape of the shell was slightly oval, with long umbones and both valves curved outward. *Inoceramus* was attached by byssal threads to the seabed or to floating material like wood. This specimen has some of its shell left, which shows as the white sections of the fossil in the photograph.

Size: About 4¾ in (12 cm) long
Distribution: Worldwide
Time range: Jurassic to Cretaceous

Spondylus

These bivalves have a very symmetrical shell—its outer edge forms a half-circle. The umbones are small and pointed, at the tip of a triangular point. There are regularly spaced growth lines and strong ribs. The shell has spines which help to anchor the bivalve to the soft seabed. These usually broke off before fossilization. You can just see the stumps where the spines once were on the specimen in the photo.

Size: Up to 4¾ in (12 cm) long
Distribution: Worldwide
Time range: Jurassic to Quaternary

Venericardia

This was a group of large bivalves with thick shells. The growth lines had wide ribs with grooves between them. The edges of the valves were notched. These bivalves lived in shallow burrows with their rear ends level to the seabed's surface. They were well-suited to life in choppy, shallow seas. Specimens are found in sandstones with other bivalves and gastropods like *Turritella* and *Natica*.

Size: Up to 6 in (15 cm) across
Distribution: North America, Africa, and Europe
Time range: Tertiary

Modiolus

These common bivalve fossils are relatives of the present-day mussel, a commonly found animal on beaches. The shell of *Modiolus* has clear growth lines and is stretched out toward the rear end. The valves are the same size and are straight where they hinge.

Size: Up to 4 in (10 cm) long
Distribution: Worldwide
Time range: Devonian to Quaternary

Pseudopecten

Members of this well-known bivalve genus were able to swim by flapping their valves. The shell had strong ribs that spread out from pointed umbones to a rounded outside edge. The shell also had growth lines. Inside each valve was a single large scar where a muscle was once attached.

Size: Up to 8 in (20 cm) across
Distribution: Europe, South America, and East Indies
Time range: Jurassic

Pholadomya

This bivalve group had very elongated shells. The valves had bold ribs and there is a gape (or gap) between the valves at the rear end. This is common in bivalves that burrow. The gape allows the siphons to reach out to the surface of the sediment, even if the shell is well dug in.

Size: Up to 4¾ in (12 cm) long
Distribution: Worldwide—Time range: Triassic to Quaternary

Gryphaea

Size: About 4 in (10 cm) long
Distribution: Worldwide
Time range: Upper Triassic to Upper Jurassic

Gryphaea was a genus of oysters, of which one species, *Gryphaea arcuata,* is shown here. The valves of this species were not the same. It had one large, heavy, and curved valve with hooked umbones, while the other valve was flatter and curved inward. The larger valve had heavy growth lines and the umbones often leaned to one side. Other species of *Gryphaea* had triangular or rounded shapes.

Trace Fossils

Body parts are not the only things left behind by organisms that can become fossilized—tracks, trails, burrows, and dung can become fossils, as well. Known as trace fossils, these types of fossils tell us about prehistoric environments and the way that ancient animals lived. Many creatures—from worms to dinosaurs—have left trace fossils.

The speed of dinosaurs

A series of fossilized footprints can be used to determine the speed of a walking or running dinosaur. The distance between the footprints is the stride. It is also possible to work out the dinosaur's height and weight and whether it walked on two or four legs from its footprints. A large animal takes long strides, while a small animal takes shorter strides. The deeper the footprint, the heavier the animal.

Walk like a dinosaur

You can stomp across a sandy beach leaving an alarming trail of dinosaur footprints. Here is how to make an outline of a track that looks like it was made by the foot of a meat-eating dinosaur. The real footprint would have been about 12 inches long and about 10 inches wide (30 by 25 centimeters) with three toes and long claws.

1 **Draw two outlines** on a piece of heavy cardboard or plywood.
2 **Cut out the cardboard,** or ask an adult to cut out the wood shapes for you.
3 **Punch four holes into each shape** (or ask an adult to drill them for you in wood) and thread a length of string through the holes. Tie the shapes to your feet. Add longer strings for your hands to make walking easier.
4 **Notice how the size of these shapes** makes you swing your legs around.

Satapliasaurus

This is the footprint of a two-legged dinosaur which roamed marshlands. It is a cast fossil that was found when the rock was split. It is not possible to work out from a footprint exactly what the dinosaur looked like.
Sometimes large numbers of footprints of different sizes are found in one place. This shows us that the dinosaurs may possibly have lived in a herd.

The specimen shown here is 6 in (15 cm) long, but some have been found up to 24 in (60 cm) long. This one is from the Middle Jurassic Period.

Make a trace fossil

You will need: a tray of damp sand, a strip of cardboard about 2 by 15 inches (5 by 35 centimeters), plaster of Paris, water, and some paper clips.

1 **Smooth the sand until it is level.** Push your hand or foot firmly into the tray to make a print.

2 **Place the cardboard strip in a ring** around the print. Paper clip it together so that it is firm and push it a little way into the sand. It should form a raised border around the print.

3 **Mix up enough plaster of Paris** to fill the mold. Pour it into the cardboard circle and fill it to just below the brim. Leave the plaster to dry.

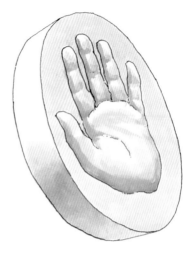

4 **When the plaster has set,** remove the cardboard strip. Lift the plaster out of the sand. You should have a cast of your hand or foot.

5 **Try making a cast of a "burrow"** as well. Make the burrow by pushing a pencil or a pipe cleaner into the sand. Then pour in plaster of Paris.

Scolicia

This long, curved fossil shows the grazing trail of a gastropod mollusk (see pages 47–51). It is preserved as a cast. Minerals have filled in the grooved trail left on the sandy seabed.
The area shown is 8 in (20 cm) across. Specimens have been found from all periods between the Cambrian and Quaternary

Coprolite

This is the fossil of a lump of turtle excrement (feces or droppings). Such fossils can tell us what kind of food an animal ate. Coprolite is the word used to describe fossilized excrement. This specimen is covered in the iron ore limonite.
This specimen is 1¼ in (3 cm) long. It comes from North America and dates from the Tertiary Period

Cephalopods

Mollusks

This group of mollusks lived—and, in fact, still live—in the sea. Unlike other mollusks, some cephalopods have shells that are divided up into chambers. Cephalopods such as ammonites and nautiloids have shells on the outside of the body, which are usually coiled. Their body is in the last chamber of the shell, near the opening, and the front part of the body, with tentacles and eyes, sticks out of the shell. The other chambers, called buoyancy chambers, contain a mixture of gas and liquid. They raise the animal off the seabed. Cephalopods such as squids, cuttlefish, and belemnites have their shell inside their bodies.

Actinoceras

These early cephalopods were nautiloids that had a straight, tube-shaped shell divided into chambers. There was a tube—the siphuncle—that reached from the body chamber through all the buoyancy chambers. The animals used this tube to alter the contents of the buoyancy chambers and thereby control their depth. This thin, broken specimen shows the chambered shell. The walls between the chambers are called septa.

Size: This specimen is 3¼ in (8 cm) long
Distribution: Worldwide
Time range: Lower Ordovician to Carboniferous

Nautilus

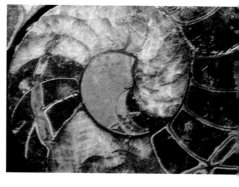

The shells of these large nautiloids have a large, outer whorl (one turn in a spiral), which partly hides the inner whorls.
The cross section of the fossil clearly shows the septa dividing the shell into chambers, and the siphuncle tube (see *Actinoceras*) passing through these chambers. A modern-day relative of the variety shown in this photo can be found in the South Pacific and Indian oceans.

Size: Up to 11 in (28 cm) across
Distribution: North America, Europe, Asia, and North Africa
Time range: Jurassic to Quaternary

Orthoceras

These extinct nautiloids had a long, slender shell which tapered, or narrowed, to a point. The chambers were divided by septa. The lines that show where the septa met the outside shell are called suture lines.

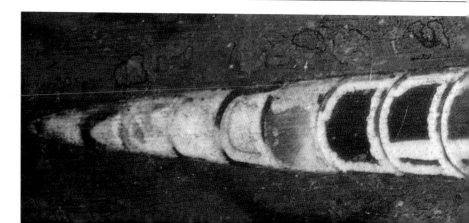

Clymenia

This early ammonoid genus had a smooth, coiled shell with faint ribs. The ribs were spread out like spokes from the hub of a wheel. The hub (or center) of an ammonite shell is called the umbilicus. *Clymenia's* whorls were loosely held together, so they can all be seen clearly on fossilized specimens. In some ammonoids, the outer whorl hides the inner ones.

Size: Up to 3¼ in (8 cm) across
Distribution: Europe, Asia, and North Africa
Time range: Devonian

Prolecanites

Most of the whorls of this ammonoid were not hidden and were narrow and flattened. In this photo, the wavy suture lines extend to the end of the last whorl, which means that the body chamber of this specimen is missing.

Size: Up to 8 in (20 cm) across
Distribution: North America, Europe, and Asia
Time range: Carboniferous

Echioceras

This was an open-coiled genus of ammonites in which all the whorls could be seen. There were thick, well-spaced ribs which spread out from the center like the spokes of a wheel. A thin ridge ran around the outside edge (not shown in photo). A species of this group, *Echioceras raricostatum*, is a zone fossil (see page 9) for part of the Lower Jurassic Period.

Size: Up to 4 in (10 cm) across
Distribution: Worldwide
Time range: Lower Jurassic

Cladiscites

The outer whorl of these medium-sized ammonoids hid the inner whorls completely. The umbilicus was very narrow. This specimen's shell is worn down, and the delicate patterning of its suture lines can be seen, but the body chamber is missing.

Size: Up to 8 in (20 cm) across
Distribution: Europe (but not the U.K.), Alaska, and the Himalaya
Time range: Triassic

These lines can only be seen when the outer shell has gone. *Orthoceras* swam near the seabed with its tentacled body pointing down and buoyant shell pointing up. Large numbers of these fossils form *Orthoceras* limestone. The long shells of specimens are often broken.

Size: The shell can be several feet (around a meter) long
Distribution: Europe
Time range: Lower Ordovician to Triassic

Cephalopods

Mollusks

Pleuroceras

The inner whorls of these ammonites could be clearly seen. In cross section, the whorls were rectangular. The shell had thick, well-spaced ribs, which sometimes had spines and lumps near the outside edge. These are often broken off in fossil specimens. Some of the shell has been lost from this specimen, but suture lines can still be seen on the whorls.

Size: Up to 4 in (10 cm) across
Distribution: Europe and North Africa
Time range: Lower Jurassic

Hildoceras

This specimen is the species *Hildoceras bifrons*. It is a zone fossil (see page 9) for part of the Lower Jurassic Period. Most of the inner whorls are showing on this specimen and the ribs are curved. Many of these fossils are found in dark shale cliffs in North Yorkshire, in the United Kingdom. The genus is named after St. Hilda, who founded an abbey in Yorkshire.

Size: About 4¾ in (12 cm) across
Distribution: Europe, Asia Minor, and Japan
Time range: Lower Jurassic

Promicroceras

This is a genus of small ammonites; all of the whorls are visible. The shell was patterned with thick ribs that spread out from a wide umbilicus, then curved and became flat as they reached the outer edge. This specimen is crowded with fossils. Some have a complete shell; others do not. Some suture lines can be seen where the shell is missing.

Size: Grew to a maximum of 1½ in (4 cm) across
Distribution: Europe—Time range: Jurassic

Asteroceras

A genus of ammonites patterned with thick, widely spaced ribs that curved forward as they reached the outside edge. In this specimen, the buoyancy chambers are filled with pale calcite. Fossils of this genus are commonly found with bivalves, such as *Gryphaea, Pholadomya,* and *Pseudopecten.* In the same rocks, sea lilies, including *Pentacrinites,* brachiopods, and trace fossil burrows (see page 39), can often be found.

Size: Up to 4 in (10 cm) across
Distribution: North America, Europe, and Asia
Time range: Lower Jurassic

Dactylioceras

An ammonite genus with all the whorls visible—each whorl is rounded in section. *Dactylioceras* had thick ribs that split into two as they reached the outer edge. Some species had rows of lumps on the inner whorls.
Size: Up to 4 in (10 cm) across
Distribution: Worldwide—Time range: Lower Jurassic

Amaltheus

This genus of ammonites had a flattened shell and hidden inner whorls. The ribs curved forward as they reach the ridged, outside edge. The ridge looks like heavy rope. Specimens of these ammonites are found in different kinds of sedimentary rock, including limestones and sandstones. In this specimen, there is sediment in the center.
Size: Up to 3¼ in (8 cm) across
Distribution: North America, Europe, North Africa, and Asia
Time range: Lower Jurassic

Lytoceras

A genus of loosely coiled ammonites with all whorls visible. The whorls were round in cross-section, getting larger toward the opening. The shell was patterned with fine ribs, which were slightly wavy at the edges of the whorls.
Size: Up to 6 in (15 cm) across
Distribution: Worldwide
Time range: Jurassic

Psiloceras

This is an important fossil group. *Psiloceras* is a zone fossil (see page 9) for the oldest zone of the Jurassic Period. Usually fossils of *Psiloceras* have been crushed flat in layers of shale, but this specimen shows a three-dimensional example. Part of the body chamber can be seen—it has no suture lines.
Size: Up to 2¾ in (7 cm) across
Distribution: Worldwide
Time range: Lower Jurassic

Cephalopods

Mollusks

In some genera of ammonites, individuals of the same species came in two sizes. The smaller of the two shells is called the microconch, and the larger is the macroconch. Some scientists believe the females may have had the large shells. This would have made it possible for the females to carry more eggs.

Acanthoscaphites

These ammonites had a slight uncoiling of the outside whorl, and the inner whorls were hidden. The shell was flattened and broad with closely spaced ribs, which curved near the center. There were swellings at the center. The opening was slightly hooked and faced the rest of the shell.
Size: Up to 2 in (5 cm) across
Distribution:
Europe, North America,
South Africa, Australia,
and Chile
Time range:
Cretaceous

Quenstedtoceras

The males and females in this genus of ammonites probably had shells of different sizes. The inner whorls were partially hidden. There were strong, curved ribs that split into two, forming a chevron (or V-shaped) pattern on the outside edge. The shell of the macroconch had less patterning.

Size: Microconch
up to 2½ in (6.5 cm);
Macroconch
up to 7 in (18 cm)
across
Distribution:
Worldwide
Time range:
Middle and Upper
Jurassic

Kosmoceras

In this genus of ammonites, the males and females probably had shells of different sizes. The microconch, shown here, had a long piece of shell, called a lappet, growing from the opening. The shell also had spines and lumps. The macroconch had no lappet.

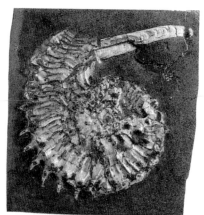

Size: About 2½ in
(6.5 cm) across
Distribution:
Worldwide
Time range:
Middle Jurassic

Cardioceras

Again, in this genus of ammonites the males and females probably had shells of different sizes. Only part of the inner whorl was visible. The main ribs split into two before they reached the outside edge. The microconch had an extra piece at the opening called a rostrum, but the macroconch did not.

Size: 2 in (5 cm) across
Distribution: Worldwide
Time range: Upper Jurassic

Parkinsonia

These common ammonites looked rather like *Dactylioceras* (see page 43), even though these two genera lived millions of years apart. The whorls of *Parkinsonia* were all visible. The shell was patterned with ribs that split into two on the outside edge. There was a slight groove running around the outside edge, which the ribs did not cross.

Size: Up to 6 in (15 cm) across
Distribution: Europe, Asia, and North Africa
Time range: Middle Jurassic

Mantelliceras

Only part of the inner whorls was visible in this ammonite group. There were thick ribs that developed two rows of lumps at the outside edge. These fossils are often found with other ammonites, and with bivalves like *Chlamys*, *Inoceramus*, *Exogyra*, and *Lopha*. The echinoid *Holaster* is also often found with *Mantelliceras*.

Size: Up to 4 in (10 cm) across
Distribution: Europe, North Africa, Asia, and North America
Time range: Cretaceous

Turrilites

This ammonite genus had a strangely shaped shell—coiled into a spiral like a gastropod (see page 47). Unlike gastropods, however, *Turrilites* had suture lines and chambers. The ribs were weak, with well-formed swellings. It probably swam with the buoyant shell on top and its tentacled body facing the seabed.

Size: Up to 6 in (15 cm) long
Distribution: Worldwide
Time range: Cretaceous

Baculites

These ammonites had a very small, coiled shell in the early stages of life. Later, the shell grew straight. The shell in specimens is often broken and only short pieces are found as fossils. This specimen shows the fine and intricate suture lines, which help to identify it as an ammonite. Sometimes *Baculites* also had ribs and swellings. There was a rostrum on one side of the opening.

Size: Up to 6½ ft (2 m) long
Distribution: Worldwide
Time range: Upper Cretaceous

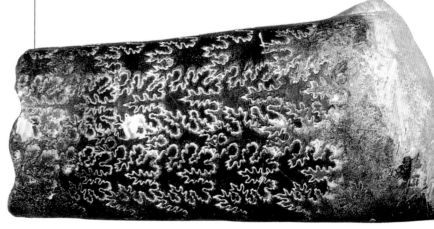

Gastropods & Others

Mollusks

Dentalium

This fossil belongs to a class of mollusks called the scaphopods. Three different species are shown in this photograph. They are all tube-shaped and usually have ribs running from top to bottom. Present-day scaphopods live on the seabed with the narrow end reaching into the water. Seawater is sucked in and pushed out at this end. At the other end, the foot and many thin arms covered with cilia stick out.

Size: Up to 2½ in (6.5 cm) long—Distribution: Worldwide
Time range: Triassic to Quaternary

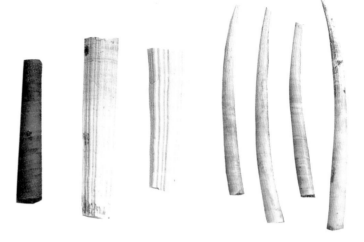

Belemnitella

This is a commonly found fossil genus of belemnites. The surface of the fossil is marked with lines and grooves, which spread apart at the pointed peak of the shell. Complete specimens may have a larger, chambered section that is joined to the wider end of the guard (inside shell). These fossils are difficult to collect because they break easily.

Size: These specimens are about 7 in (18 cm) long
Distribution: North America, Europe, Asia, and Greenland
Time range: Upper Cretaceous

Acrocoelites

These are also called belemnites—squidlike creatures that had tentacles and eyes. Belemnites are cephalopods, as are the ammonites. Belemnites belong to a class which includes squids, octopods, and cuttlefish. The fossils found are bullet-shaped and consist of the inside shell. The photograph shows a mass of fossils all arranged in the same direction. They may have been swept into this configuration by a strong current.

Size: Up to 4¾ in (12 cm) long
Distribution: Europe and North America
Time range: Lower Jurassic

Present-day gastropods include snails, slugs, limpets, and whelks. Most gastropods have an outside shell that is coiled in a spiral. The body of the animal is in the last, and usually largest, whorl, next to the opening. The animal pokes its head and fleshy foot out of this opening. There is sometimes a groove on the opening, called the siphonal notch, which draws water to the gills. Gastropods live in fresh water, at sea, and on land.

Poleumita

The coiled shell of these gastropods had a flattened upper surface. In the center of each whorl was a prominent ridge. The shell was marked by fine lines, which spread out across it from the center. There were sometimes small spines. *Poleumita* is found in sediments laid down in shallow seawater.

Size: Up to 1½ in (4 cm) across
Distribution: North America and Europe
Time range: Silurian

Straparollus

These were gastropods with a coiled shell that was either a high spiral or flat. The shell was smooth but had many thin ribs spreading out across the whorls. There was a slight flat-topped ridge running along the center of each whorl. These fossils are found preserved in limestones formed in shallow seawater and on the slopes of reefs.

Size: Up to 2 in (5 cm) across
Distribution: Worldwide
Time range: Silurian to Permian

Mourlonia

These gastropods had a spire-shaped shell that ended in a narrow, rounded point, or apex. The whorls became wider and flatter toward the opening. The sutures (or joining lines) between the whorls were thin. The shell had a pattern of thin spiraling ribs. *Mourlonia* crawled on the seabed in very shallow water.

Size: Up to 1½ in (4 cm) across
Distribution: Worldwide
Time range: Ordovician to Permian

Gastropods & Others

Mollusks

Conotomaria

These cone-shaped fossils had whorls with only shallow sutures between them. The base of the shell was flat. The shell was marked with spiraling lines and low ridges. This specimen is an internal cast fossil (see page 8). *Conotomaria* lived and crawled on the seabed. It is found with other fossils, including bivalves and ammonites.

Size: Up to 6 in (15 cm) tall
Distribution: Worldwide
Time range: Middle Jurassic to Tertiary

Ficus

Ficus was a pear-shaped gastropod with a large body whorl. This whorl covered most of the other whorls; only the pointed apex was visible. At the other end, the opening again tapered to a narrow base. The shell was marked by curved lines. *Ficus* lived in shallow seas and is often fossilized with other gastropods like *Turritella*.

Size: Up to 4 in (10 cm) long
Distribution: Worldwide
Time range: Tertiary to Quaternary

Bourguetia

These sea snails lived in shallow seas and were quite large gastropods. They had large, heavy shells, which tapered to a blunt apex. The whorls were smooth, although there may have been thin growth lines. This specimen has many small, round marks on the shell. These were made by ooliths, spherical grains of the oolitic limestone in which the shell was preserved.

Size: Up to 4 in (10 cm) long
Distribution: Europe
Time range: Middle and Upper Jurassic

Pleurotomaria

Examples of this group of sea-living gastropods are often preserved with ammonites, belemnites, bivalves, brachiopods, and corals. The whorls of *Pleurotomaria* were coiled in a low spiral that became larger toward the opening, which was large and flared. The shell was marked with growth lines, lumps, and bands. There were deep grooves, or "sutures," between the whorls.
Size: Up to 4¾ in (12 cm) tall—Distribution: Worldwide
Time range: Jurassic to Cretaceous

Cerithium

These gastropods had a long, slender, cone-shaped shell with many small whorls. Each whorl had a ridge covered with small spines and lumps. There were spiraling growth lines which formed an S-shape on the final body whorl. The small opening was pear-shaped. These specimens have been preserved in clay formed on the seabed.
Size: Up to 1¼ in (3 cm) long
Distribution: Worldwide
Time range: Upper Cretaceous to Quaternary

Rimella

This was a group of sea-living gastropods with cornet-shaped shells. The spire tapered to a point. The opening had a long siphonal canal that stretched to the apex. (This is on the underside of the specimen shown.) The shell had a pattern of curved ribs.
Size: Up to 1¼ in (3 cm) long
Distribution: Worldwide
Time range: Upper Tertiary

Sycostoma

These sea-living gastropods had a large, tapering body whorl, followed by other whorls that formed a cone. The shell ended in a rounded apex. There was a slight ridge following each suture, and the surface of the shell was marked by ribs and thin, encircling lines.
Size: Up to 2¾ in (7 cm) tall
Distribution: Worldwide
Time range: Upper Cretaceous to Tertiary

Gastropods & Others

Mollusks

Ancilla

These gastropods have a smooth shell with thin sutures. The body whorl is much larger than those of other gastropods, which usually end in a sharp apex. The opening is large and there is a wide siphonal notch. (These are on the underside of the specimen shown.) The surface of the shell remains shiny only if preservation is very good.
Size: Up to 2 in (5 cm) long
Distribution:
Worldwide
Time range:
Upper Cretaceous to Quaternary

Natica

These gastropods kill and eat other shellfish. *Natica* first softens the shells of its prey with acid from a special gland. It uses its teeth to drill a hole through the shell and then sucks out the soft body inside. *Natica*'s shell is thick and dome-shaped. The body whorl is very large, and its outer wall overlaps the other whorls. There is an operculum (or lid) covering the opening, which is often missing in fossil specimens.
Size: Up to 1¼ in (3 cm) tall
Distribution:
Worldwide
Time range:
Cretaceous to
Quaternary

Planorbis

Planorbis has a small, round shell which curves inward on one side and is flatter on the other. It looks like an ammonite, except that ammonites curve inward on both sides. *Planorbis* breathes using a simple lung. This specimen has a smooth surface with faint growth lines. Present-day members of this genus live in still and running fresh water and feed on algae and other plants.
Size: Up to 1¼ in (3 cm) across—Distribution: Worldwide
Time range: Tertiary to Quaternary

Crucibulum

This fossil belongs to a genus of gastropods known as slipper limpets. Their thick shell is pyramid-shaped and completely open at the base. Modern members of this group begin life as males and turn into females after three years. They then become less active and stick themselves to dead shells or rocks.
Size: Up to 2 in (5 cm) tall
Distribution: North America,
West Indies, and Europe
Time range: Tertiary to Quaternary

Turritella

This genus of gastropod has a long, narrow, screw-shaped shell. The whorls overlap slightly, and there are deep sutures between them. The opening is almost square in shape. The shell is patterned with growth lines, which spiral around it. Present-day members of this group burrow into the seabed with the apex pointing down, and the opening held just above the surface of the sediment.

Size: Up to 2 in (5 cm) long
Distribution: Worldwide
Time range: Cretaceous to Quaternary

Volutospina

This average-sized gastropod had a large body whorl that tapered to a narrow base; the other whorls spiraled to a point. The whorls had ridges, or shoulders, which were covered with pointed bumps. The shell had strong ribs and growth lines.

Size: Up to 4¾ in (12 cm) long
Distribution: Worldwide
Time range: Upper Cretaceous to Quaternary

Conus

Species of *Conus* have a shell that tapers to a point at both ends. There is a large body whorl and a long, narrow opening; the other whorls form a pyramid shape. There are growth lines with bumps running around the shell. The group is often fossilized in great numbers, as shown here. Present-day members of *Conus* live in warm seas—such as in the Indo-Pacific region and off northern Australia.

Size: Up to 4 in (10 cm) long
Distribution: Worldwide
Time range: Upper Cretaceous to Quaternary

A collection of fossils is more enjoyable and more valuable to science if it is well organized. It feels good to see the results of your hard work on display, and it's useful to be able to call up information about the specimens quickly.

You might like to keep a diary, recording when and where you find your fossils. Take your field notebook with you when you go fossil hunting. Make sketches of the area and its fossils for your diary.

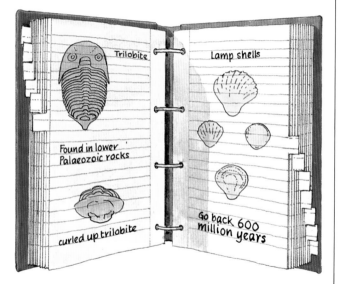

Trilobite

Lamp shells

Found in lower Palaeozoic rocks

curled up trilobite

Go back 600 million years

A fossil diary

Keep your diary in a loose-leaf binder on separate sheets of paper. Fill out a sheet for each fossil-hunting trip with the details from your field notebook. You can also write notes in your diary whenever you visit a museum or see a television program about fossils. You can decorate the diary with your own drawings, or with photographs, pictures from magazines, postcards, and so on. You will need: large sheets of colored stiff paper, a ruler, a pencil, a pair of scissors, a felt-tip pen.

1 **Cut the sheets of stiff paper (called card) into 12 pages** that are the same height as the notebook pages, but half an inch wider.

Organizing your collection

You may want to put special or delicate specimens in a glass-fronted cabinet. This will protect your specimens from damage and dust. The rest of your collection can be kept in individual trays in a drawer or shallow box.

1 **Number each fossil and keep a card index file or set up a spreadsheet file** with information about every specimen. Be sure to include the date, the exact location where the fossil was found, and the kind of rock formation in which it was found. The numbers on the cards or spreadsheet entries should correspond with the numbers on the specimen.

2 **Put a small patch of correction fluid** on to an unimportant part of each fossil. Then carefully inscribe the fossil's number.

2 **Divide the height of the card pages** into 12. On the first page cut away $^{11}/_{12}$ths of the ½ inch margin, leaving the last 12th at the top to form a tag.

3 **On the second card page,** cut away $^{11}/_{12}$ths of the margin, but this time leave the tag $^{1}/_{12}$th down from the top.

4 **Repeat this 10 times,** each time leaving the tag in a different position.

5 **Write 1 of the 12 months of the year** onto each of the 12 tags. When you put these card pages into your file, they will act as dividers. If you have positioned the tags in the right way, they should not overlap.

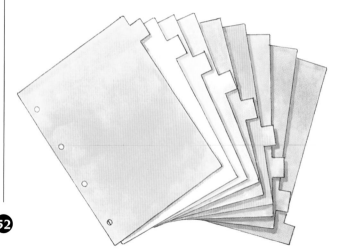

3 **If you make trays for your fossils,** you can adjust the dividers to fit the specimens. Or you can reuse the Styrofoam egg-packing trays discarded by grocery stores.

4 **Line each tray with cotton** for added protection and place a small label card in each tray. This card could just include the name of the fossil, its number, and where it was found.

Keeping a record

Your computer or a card index file should give detailed information about each fossil, such as:
- the fossil's number
- its name, if known, or the group to which it belongs
- the date it was found
- where it was found, with a name and description of the place, and map references
- the type of rock in which it was found
- recognizable features nearby the find, like a cave or a hill
- the weather on the day of your visit

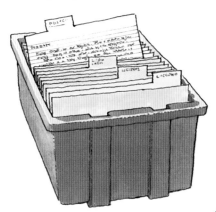

A home for your collection

You will need: some shoe boxes (with lids) and some stiff paper.

1 **Measure the box** across its short side and its depth. Draw a rectangle **(A)** on the card to match (e.g. 6 by 5 in [15 by 13 cm]). Draw two lines across the rectangle to divide it into three.

2 **Measure the long side** (e.g. 12 by 15 in [30 by 37 cm]). Draw another rectangle **(B)** to match this size. Draw two lines across it to divide it into three.

3 **Cut out each rectangle;** then cut another one each of **(B)** and **(A)**, using the first rectangles as patterns. You could have extra partitions.

4 **Pad the bottom of the box** with cotton if you like. Then cut halfway up each dividing line of each partition and slot them together as shown. Last, slide the partitions into the box.

5 **Paint the boxes and their lids** with latex paint so that they match. Ask permission, though!

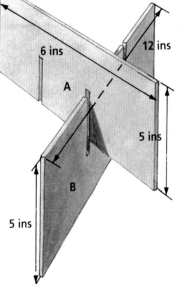

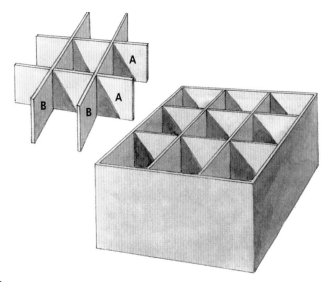

Trilobites

Arthropods

Trilobites were sea-dwelling and belonged to a large phylum of animals known as the arthropods. This group includes spiders and insects, scorpions, crabs, and lobsters. The trilobites lived for a time span of about 300 million years, becoming extinct in the Permian Period.

The trilobite's exoskeleton, or outside shell, was made of jointed segments. To grow, the animal had to molt (shed) this exoskeleton. One trilobite could therefore leave behind several shells that could fossilize. Trilobites' exoskeletons were in three sections: the head-shield, or cephalon; the tail-shield, or pygidium; and a middle section, called the thorax. From head to tail, the body was also divided into three lobes (or sections). The middle lobe is called the axis. The middle lobe of the cephalon is called the glabella.

Size: Up to 1½ in (4 cm) long
Distribution: Europe
Time range: Ordovician

Ogyginus

The cephalon and pygidium of this trilobite group were the same size. There was a large glabella surrounded by oval-shaped eyes. Genal spines extend a short way along the thorax. These are often broken off, but they can be seen in this specimen. The thoracic axis continued to the pygidium, then tapered rapidly. There were eight thoracic segments.

Ogygopsis

These trilobites had a long, deeply furrowed glabella in the center of the head-shield and many thoracic segments. The axis tapered toward the pygidium, which was larger than the cephalon and had a narrow border around it. Short genal spines (see *Olenellus*) are present in undamaged fossil specimens of *Ogygopsis*.
Size: Up to 3¼ in (8 cm) long
Distribution: North America—Time range: Cambrian

Olenellus

These medium-sized trilobites had a wide cephalon and a furrowed glabella. There were large, crescent-shaped eyes at the edge of the glabella. The thoracic axis narrowed to a point and became a tail-spine. The thoracic segments had spines, and there were two spines on the cephalon, called genal spines.
Size: Up to 3¼ in (8 cm) long
Distribution: North America, Greenland, and northern Scotland
Time range: Cambrian

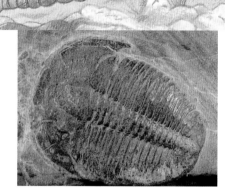

Elrathia

These trilobites had a cephalon wider than the thorax. There were two short genal spines (see *Olenellus*) on the cephalon and a short, oval-shaped glabella. The eyes were sometimes joined to the glabella by small ridges. The thoracic axis narrows toward the small pygidium. There were 12 to 17 thoracic segments.

Size: Up to 1¼ in (3 cm) long
Distribution: North America
Time range: Cambrian

Peronopsis

This was a group of very small, blind trilobites with only two thoracic segments. The cephalon and pygidium were equal in size and had borders.

Size: Up to ¼ in (0.5 cm) long
Distribution: North America, Europe, and Siberia
Time range: Cambrian

Trinucleus

These small trilobites featured a large cephalon and a lump on the front of the glabella. The cephalon had a wide border with grooves. There were long genal spines, which stretched past the six thoracic segments to the pygidium. *Trinucleus* is found in fine-grained sediment formed in deep seas and is often found with the trilobite *Ogygiocarella* (see page 56.)

Size: Up to 1¼ in (3 cm) long
Distribution: Europe
Time range: Ordovician

Paradoxides

One of the largest trilobites, *Paradoxides* had a thorax of over 15 segments. These segments had ribs on the outer surface that often narrowed to a point; they could have spines. The pygidium was small. The glabella was large and had large, curved eyes.

Size: Up to 20 in (51 cm) long
Distribution: Europe, North and South America, Turkey, and North Africa.
Time range: Cambrian

Trilobites

Arthropods

Phacops

These trilobites featured many small lumps on the cephalon and thoracic axis. *Phacops* had large, kidney-shaped eyes. The thorax had 11 segments. The axis narrowed only slightly before reaching the pygidium, but it then narrowed rapidly. Commonly found in mudstones, shales, and sandstones, fossils of this trilobite are often found lying in a curled-up position.

Size: Up to 2 in (5 cm) long
Distribution: North America, Europe, and North Africa
Time range: Silurian to Devonian

Calymene

This specimen shows the trilobite curled up. Most trilobites were able to do this, and it may have been a form of defense. The head of the trilobite in the photo is in the center, with the body curled around it. *Calymene*'s triangular cephalon had a large glabella, with four rounded bumps. The thorax had 12 segments. The axis reached the pygidium, which had 6 segments.

Size: Up to 4 in (10 cm) long
Distribution: North and South America, Australia, and Europe
Time range: Silurian to Devonian

Dalmanites

These trilobites had a large, semicircular cephalon with genal spines. There were large eyes raised high on the head-shield, so *Dalmanites* could see horizontally in all directions at once. This was good protection from attackers. *Dalmanites*'s small pygidium had a long tail-spine. There was also a spine on the cephalon. This spine may have been used to stir up sediment on the sea floor to find food.

Size: Up to 3¼ in (8 cm) long
Distribution: North America, Europe, Russia, and Australia
Time range: Silurian to Devonian

Ogygiocarella

This trilobite may also be seen in books and displays under the name *Ogygiocaris*. It had a broad cephalon with long genal spines. The glabella reached to the edge of the cephalon, and there were crescent-shaped eyes. The thorax had eight segments. The axis hardly narrowed at all at the thorax but then narrowed rapidly at the pygidium.

Size: Up to 3¼ in (8 cm) long
Distribution: Europe and South America
Time range: Ordovician

Triarthrus

Specimens of *Triarthrus* with preserved soft parts have been found in North America. These parts include antennae and walking and gill-bearing limbs. *Triarthrus*'s thorax had 12 to 16 segments. The small, triangular pygidium had 5 segments. The cephalon was semicircular with wide borders. The glabella was segmented, with very small eyes.

Size: Up to 1¼ in (3 cm) long
Distribution: Worldwide
Time range: Ordovician

Illaenus

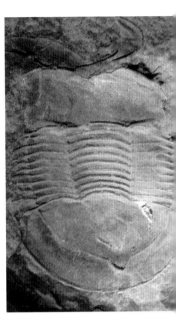

This is a genus of trilobites that had a cephalon and pygidium of the same size. Both were smooth, broad, and semicircular. The pygidium had no segments, but it did have a deep groove that followed the outline of the exoskeleton. The glabella is not easy to see in fossilized forms, but there were large, crescent-shaped eyes. The thorax had 10 segments.

Size: Up to 2 in (5 cm) long
Distribution: Worldwide
Time range: Ordovician

Bumastus

Species of *Bumastus* had a short thorax with 10 segments. The cephalon and pygidium were large, rounded, and smooth. The eyes were far on the side of the glabella. Specimens of this trilobite are sometimes found curled up. Fossils of *Bumastus* are found in limestones formed in shallow waters with corals, crinoids, brachiopods, and mollusks.

Size: Up to 4 in (10 cm) long
Distribution: North America and Europe
Time range: Silurian

Trimerus

This trilobite had an unusual thorax with no clear lobes. The axis was wide and the segments smooth. The pygidium was triangular and had an axis, which narrowed to a point. There were no eyes. These characteristics make scientists think that *Trimerus* may have been a burrower.

Size: Up to 8 in (20 cm) long
Distribution: Worldwide
Time range: Silurian to Devonian

Other Arthropods

Pterygotus

This slender, scorpionlike creature lived in ancient times in seas or brackish water. Its body was segmented. The thorax narrowed to a tail, which may have had spines. From the cephalon (see page 54) grew limbs that carried large, strong claws. There were also three additional pairs of paddle-shaped limbs and large eyes, which suggests that *Pterygotus* was probably a fast-moving hunter.

Size: Up to 5 ft (1.5 m) long, but usually only about 8 in (20 cm) long
Distribution: All continents except Africa and Antarctica
Time range: Ordovician to Devonian

Mesolimulus

This is an ancestor of the horseshoe crabs that live today. The cephalon of *Mesolimulus* was large and semicircular and had genal spines (see page 54). The thorax was short and triangular, and the pygidium ended in a long tail-spine. There were five pairs of walking limbs and one pair of pincers.
Size: Up to 10 in (25 cm) long
Distribution: Europe
Time range: Triassic to Cretaceous

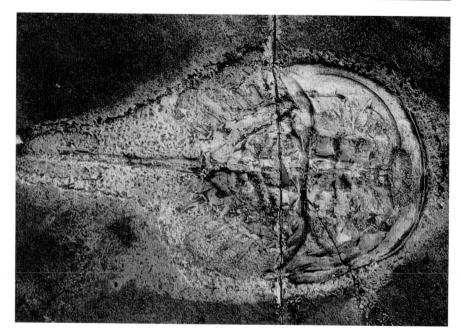

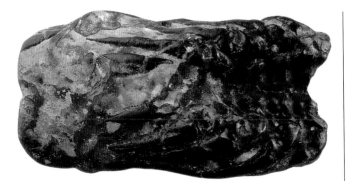

Hoploparia

This extinct lobster had many points of similarity with present-day lobsters. The specimen shown here is incomplete, but its segmented legs can be seen.
Size: Specimen is 2½ in (6.5 cm) long
Distribution: Worldwide
Time range: Tertiary

Euestheria

The carapace (or shell) of this creature looks like that of a bivalve mollusk. In fact, this animal was a crustacean, belonging to a class known as Branchiopoda. The carapace was marked by growth lines, which were left by molting. *Euestheria* lived in fresh water.
Size: Up to ½ in (1 cm) long—Distribution: Worldwide
Time range: Triassic to Jurassic

Libellula

This is the delicate fossil of a dragonfly larva—the second stage of the dragonfly life cycle—preserved in very fine-grained limestone. This kind of preservation can only happen when the soft sediment was laid down quickly in gentle conditions.
Size: This specimen is ½ in (1 cm) long
Distribution: Worldwide
Time range: Triassic to Quaternary

Glyphea

A member of the order that includes lobsters and shrimps, *Glyphea* had five pairs of limbs, which are not often preserved in fossil form. Its carapace was rough, with a surface that was covered with small pits. The head had eyes and feelers. Fossils of *Glyphea* are often found with trace fossils of burrows known as *Thalassinoides* (see page 39), perhaps *Glyphea* made these burrows.
Size: Up to 1¾ in (4.5 cm) long
Distribution: North America, Europe, Greenland, East Africa, and Australia
Time range: Triassic to Cretaceous

Brachiopods

Other Invertebrates

These sea-living creatures are still found in oceans today; they have shells made up of two valves. Unlike bivalves, however, the valves are not the same size. In brachiopods, there is a larger valve—called a pedicle valve—which has a hole in it. A fleshy stalk, called a pedicle, sticks out of this hole and fixes the brachiopod to the seabed or the base of a burrow. The smaller valve is called the brachial valve.

Leptaena

These were articulate brachiopods (meaning they could open and close their valves). Their shell had a semicircular outline. The valves were straight where hinged. The pedicle valve curved outward and the brachial valve was flat. *Leptaena* lay on the sea floor with the brachial valve uppermost.
Size: Up to 2 in (5 cm) wide
Distribution: Worldwide
Time range: Ordovician to Devonian

Lingula

This is a group of inarticulate brachiopods, which means that they cannot move their valves. The outline of the shell of this species is oval and the valves are patterned with many thin ribs and growth lines. *Lingula* burrows into the seabed and has a pedicle as long as the shell. This is one of the longest-surviving groups of brachiopods.
Size: Up to 1¼ in (3 cm) long
Distribution: Worldwide
Time range: Ordovician to Quaternary

Schizophoria

This group of articulate brachiopods had an almost oblong outline. Both valves curved outward, but the brachial valve curved more. Both valves are shown; the pedicle valve is on the left
Size: Up to 2 in (5 cm) wide
Distribution: Worldwide
Time range: Silurian to Permian

Spirifer

These articulate brachiopods had a semicircular outline with a straight hinge line—the hinge was on the widest part of the shell. The umbo of the pedicle valve can be seen sticking up above the hinge line in this photo. The valves had bold ribs and growth lines. There was a fold on the brachial valve (facing out in photo), which ran from the umbo to the edge.

**Size: Up to 4¾ in
(12 cm) wide
Distribution: Worldwide
Time range: Carboniferous**

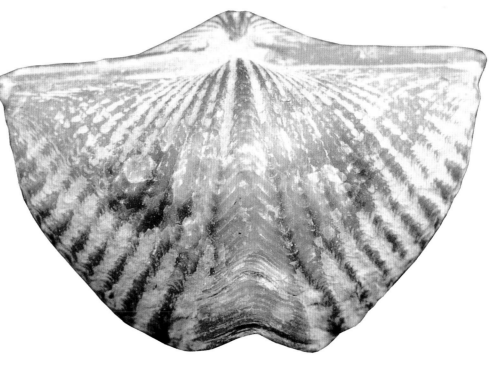

Pustula

These articulate brachiopods were almost oblong in outline and had a straight hinge line. The umbo on each valve was small and pointed. There were faint ribs and growth lines that followed the outline of the shell. The pedicle valve (facing out in photo) curved outward, the brachial valve was flat.

**Size: Up to 4¾ in
(12 cm) wide
Distribution: Europe
Time range: Carboniferous**

Brachiopods

Other Invertebrates

Productus

This genus of articulate brachiopods lay on the seabed with their brachial valves uppermost. The pedicle valve curved outward; the brachial valve was flat or curved inward. There were wavy growth lines on the surface. The shell once had spines which would have attached it to the seabed, but these are usually broken off in fossil specimens.
Size: Up to 1½ in (4 cm) wide
Distribution: Europe and Asia
Time range: Carboniferous

Tetrarhynchia

Large numbers of these articulate brachiopods in fossil form are often found preserved together in "nests." Both valves curved outward and were patterned with strong ribs that met at a zigzag fold. The umbones were small, pointed, and curved.
Size: Up to ¾ in (2 cm) wide
Distribution: North America and Europe
Time range: Jurassic

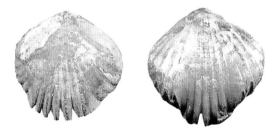

Cyclothyris

These were articulate brachiopods (meaning they could open and close their valves). These valves were triangular in shape, and both of them curved outward and were patterned with ribs and growth lines. The brachial valve had a fold, and the valves met at a zigzag line.
Size: Up to 1¼ in (3 cm) wide
Distribution: North America and Europe
Time range: Cretaceous

Terebratella

In the photograph of this articulate brachiopod, the brachial valve is facing out. The pedicle valve sticks out beyond the brachial valve, and you can see the pedicle opening. The valves of *Terebratella* are patterned with ribs that spread out from the umbo. Some ribs divide into two. There are also growth lines.

Size: Up to 1½ in (4 cm) wide
Distribution: Worldwide
Time range: Jurassic to Quaternary

Plectothyris

The shell of this articulate brachiopod was round in outline, but became triangular near the umbone. The pedicle opening was large. There were ribs only at the edge of the shell, which was smooth elsewhere. These ribs started to develop only as the animal grew older. *Plectothyris* lived fixed to the seabed, alone or in groups.

Size: Up to 1½ in (4 cm) wide
Distribution: United Kingdom
Time range: Jurassic

Pygope

These articulate brachiopods were triangular. On the brachial valve, there was a groove in the center that developed into a hole. The animal squirted water out of its shell through this hole. This water would have been sucked into the shell through holes in the side, allowing the animal to extract food and oxygen. *Pygope* was fixed to the seabed by its pedicle, which grew out of a large opening.

Size: Up to 3¼ in (8 cm) on each side
Distribution: Europe
Time range: Cretaceous

Graptolites

Other Invertebrates

These small, compound, sea-living creatures are now extinct. Groups of graptolites lived in colonies, but the individual animals lived in cuplike growths called thecae that were arranged on branching structures called rhabdosomes.

A single branch of these rhabdosome structures is known as a stipe. Early graptolites lived on the seabed, but later forms drifted in the sea currents.

Dictyonema

These are early graptolites. The rhabdosome was made up of many branches. When alive, this structure formed a cone-shaped net. The branches were joined together by weblike growths.

Size: From ¾–10 in (2–25.5 cm) long
Distribution: Worldwide
Time range: Cambrian to Carboniferous

Didymograptus

These graptolites were made up of two stipes joined together in a V-shape. The thecae were tube-shaped and formed on only one side of the stipe. *Didymograptus* drifted in sea currents. Fossils of this genus are sometimes found in great numbers, especially in shales and mudstones. Specimens are delicate and are found only in rocks with very fine grains.

Size: From ¾–24 in (2–60 cm) long
Distribution: Worldwide
Time range: Ordovician

Phyllograptus

These graptolites were made up of four stipes that looked like leaves. These stipes are usually preserved alone or in pairs. The thecae were tube-shaped and faced upward. Fossils of *Phyllograptus* are often found in black shales. The photograph shows the fossil of a single stipe.
Size: Up to 1½ in (4 cm) long
Distribution: Worldwide
Time range: Lower Ordovician

Climacograptus

These graptolites had S-shaped thecae with openings that faced upward. The thecae were arranged on both sides of a single stipe. This genus probably drifted in the sea currents in an upright position.
Size: Usually about 2 in (5 cm) long
Distribution: Worldwide
Time range: Ordovician to Silurian

Monograptus

This graptolite had a single stipe that was usually straight, but was sometimes curved or coiled. The thecae were arranged on one side of the stipe only and varied in shape from simple cups to hook-shaped or S-shaped. *Monograptus* is the most common Silurian graptolite and can sometimes be found fossilized in large numbers.
Size: From 1¼–30 in (3–76 cm) long
Distribution: Worldwide
Time range: Silurian to Devonian

Vertebrates

A vertebrate is an animal with a spinal column (backbone) and a cranium (brain case). There are eight classes of vertebrates: hagfish; lampreys; sharks and similar fish; bony fish; frogs and other amphibians; reptiles; birds; and mammals.

The first vertebrates were small animals that probably appeared at the end of the Cambrian Period, more than 500 million years ago (mya). These animals had jawless mouths, like modern-day lampreys. During the Silurian Period, starting 440 mya, vertebrates developed jaws and teeth. A great surge in the development of fishes occurred during the Devonian Period, which began about 410 mya.

About 360 mya, the first amphibians developed when lungfish (which still exist today) learned how to survive out of water. Amphibians were the dominant (ruling) group on land in the Carboniferous Period (360–286 mya).

Amphibians lay their eggs in water and their young develop there. However, reptiles lay their eggs on land and these eggs hatch into miniature adults. The first reptiles appeared during the Carboniferous Period. They resembled lizards, had sharp teeth, and ate insects.

Fish, amphibians, and reptiles are cold-blooded, while birds and mammals are warm-blooded. Some reptiles that are now extinct were probably also warm-blooded. These may have included some dinosaurs. The bodies of warm-blooded animals maintain about the same internal temperature, even if the temperature of their surroundings changes.

Mammals first appeared in the Triassic Period (248–213 mya) but were small and few in number. It is only at the start of the Tertiary Period (about 65 mya), after the dinosaurs and many invertebrates died out in some kind of catastrophe, that modern birds and mammals became the dominant groups.

Fish

Vertebrates

The most commonly found fossils of vertebrate animals (animals with backbones) are those of fish. This is because fish live in water. Water carries large amounts of sediments, and the bodies of dead animals that lived in the water can be quickly covered up and preserved by the sediment. This process is the most common way in which fossils are formed.

Cephalaspis

This fish had a large head-shield, which curved backward into two points. There were small eye-holes in the middle of the upper surface of the head shield. The fish had a small mouth on the underside of its head and probably ate by sifting food from the lake or river sediment. Water flowed into the mouth and out through slits behind it. The fish took oxygen from this water with its gills. The body was long and eellike.

Size: Up to 4 in (10 cm) long
Distribution: Worldwide
Time range: Upper Silurian to Middle Devonian

Gyroptychius

This fossil shown at right is almost a complete specimen. The body of *Gyroptychius* was covered with small, diamond-shaped scales, but the head was armored with larger plates. The fish also had two sets of paired fins toward the back of the body and a stumpy tail.

Size: This specimen is 2¾ in (7 cm) long
Distribution: Worldwide
Time range: Devonian

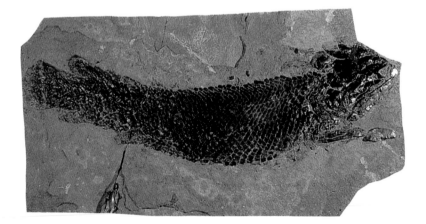

Gosiutichthys

The fish fossils in this photo have been preserved in a slab of fine-grained sediment. The fish died when the lake in which they were living dried up. *Gosiutichthys* belongs to a group of fish known as the teleosts. These fish have bony skeletons and jaws, and bony rays to support their fins. Today, about 23,000 species, which is about 95 percent of all known kinds of fish, are teleosts.

Size: Up to 20 in (51 cm) long
Distribution: North America
Time range: Tertiary

Fish

Acrolepis

This specimen has been well preserved in fine-grained sediment, although part of the head and tail are missing. *Acrolepis* was a large fish with coarse, diamond-shaped scales. The head was about one-fourth of the total length of the fish.

Size: Up to 16 in (40 cm) long
Distribution: Europe, Africa, and Greenland
Time range: Carboniferous to Permian

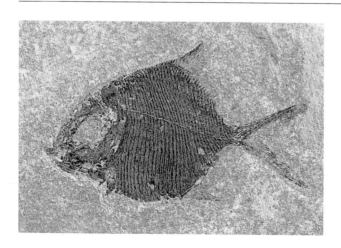

Platysomus

This specimen is very well preserved in fine-grained limestone. *Platysomus* had cone-shaped teeth and a deep body; this body was covered with scales that were longer from top to bottom than they were wide. The fins were triangular and not in pairs. *Platysomus* breathed with gills and was probably an agile swimmer.

Size: This specimen is 2¾ in (7 cm) long
Distribution: Europe
Time range: Lower Carboniferous to Upper Permian

Bothriolepis

The photograph shows the body and head of this fish. Armored plates protected the head and the front of the fish's body from attackers.Two long, curved spines extended from the front of the body plates. The rest of the body was eellike and had no scales. *Bothriolepis* lived on the muddy bottoms of freshwater lakes.

Size: This specimen is 3½ in (9 cm) long.
Distribution: Worldwide – Time range: Devonian

Leptolepis

This is an early type of bony fish. *Leptolepis* was a small fish with a long body that narrowed toward the tail. The tail had two lobes that were the same size. The small mouth was equipped with many teeth.

Size: Up to 4¾ in (12 cm) long
Distribution: North America, Europe, Asia, and South Africa
Time range: Upper Triassic to Cretaceous

Dapedius

These fish belong to a group known as the holosteans.The bodies of holosteans are covered with bony plates rather than scales. *Dapedius* had small rectangular plates on its body and larger ones on its head. It had a rounded outline and a long, dorsal fin on its back. The short tail was fan-shaped and there was a long fin below it. The mouth was small and filled with thin, sharp teeth.

Size: Up to 8 in (20 cm) long
Distribution: Europe
Time range: Lower Jurassic

Fossil Teeth

Vertebrates

Ptychodus

The specimen in the photo is the flat tooth of a shark. Such teeth were probably used to crush bivalves, ammonites, and gastropods. *Ptychodus* came from a successful group of sharks that existed for tens of millions of years.

Size: This specimen is 1¾ in (4.5 cm) long
Distribution: North America, Europe, Africa, and Asia
Time range: Cretaceous

Odontaspis

These are the teeth of an ancient shark. It has relatives alive today, which reach a length of over 13 feet (4 meters). The teeth had side cusps, seen as small, sharp points near the base of the tooth, which were made of tough material. They were easily preserved, though they are often found broken.

Size: Average shown ¾ in (2 cm) long
Distribution: North and South America, Europe, Asia, Africa, and New Zealand
Time range: Cretaceous to Quaternary

Merycoidodon

This fossil is formed from several teeth and part of the jaw of a plant-eating mammal that is also called *Oreodon*. It was a small, piglike creature with wide molar teeth, like those of cattle, and large upper canine teeth. Four species of this genus have been identified.

Size: This specimen is 2¾ in (7 cm) long
Distribution: North America
Time range: Tertiary

Ceratodus

The black area in the center of the photo is the teeth of a lungfish. The teeth were fused together into flattened plates, which helped the fish to crush the shelled creatures on which it fed. The surface of the teeth was covered with many small dimples. Like present-day lungfish, *Ceratodus* used gills to breathe when underwater, but out of the water it used a lunglike bladder.

Size: This specimen is ¾ in (2 cm) long
Distribution: Worldwide
Time range: Triassic to Cretaceous

Hyena

(Hyaena spelaea)

This is part of the lower jaw of a cave hyena. The teeth are shaped for cutting flesh and crushing bones. Present-day hyenas live in burrows and caves; they sometimes feed on animals that have already died. They also hunt animals and eat plants.

Size: This specimen is 3¼ in (8 cm) long
Distribution: Europe, North America, Africa, and Asia
Time range: Tertiary to Quaternary

Charcarodon

The teeth are the only part of this very large shark which were preserved. These fossil teeth are triangular, with two long roots at the base and jagged edges for cutting flesh. A present-day relative of this shark is the great white shark, which can grow to more than 21 feet (6.4 meters) in length. A shark that long may weigh 3 tons (3,000 kilograms) and have a biting pressure of 20 tons per square inch (2,800 kilograms per square centimeter). *Charcarodon* was probably twice as large as a great white shark.

Size: Tooth specimens up to 6 in (15 cm) long
Distribution: Worldwide
Time range: Tertiary

Mammuthus

The photograph shows the cheek tooth of this large elephantlike mammal. The surface is covered with many rough ridges and furrows, which tells us *Mammuthus* was probably a plant-eater. *Mammuthus* was adapted to living in cold conditions—it had a thick coat, a store of food in the form of a hump of fat, small ears, and a large body. These animals were hunted by prehistoric people and images of them are found in prehistoric cave paintings.

Size: This specimen is 10 in (25.5 cm) long
Distribution: North America, Europe, Asia, and Africa
Time range: Tertiary to Quaternary

Reptiles & Amphibians

Vertebrates

Fossils of large reptiles or amphibians are not very common. Some select areas have a large number of vertebrate fossils. Further, it is possible to find single teeth and bones—this is especially true of the large, sea-living reptiles. And, large dinosaur skeletons are occasionally found by amateur fossil collectors.

Iguanodon

Adult iguanodons walked on all fours. The front legs were shorter than the strong, back legs. It is thought that these animals lived in herds and were plant-eaters. *Iguanodon* had a horny, beaklike mouth and grinding teeth on both sides of the jaw. *Iguanodon* teeth were first found in England in 1822 by Mary Ann Mantell. The top specimen in the photograph is a toe bone, and the bottom specimen is part of the dinosaur's backbone.

Size: Adults grew to about 30 ft (9 m) in length
Distribution: Worldwide, except Antarctica
Time range: Cretaceous

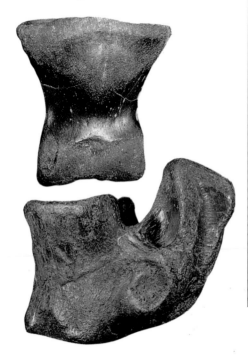

Plesiosaurus

This sea-living reptile grew to about 15 to 40 feet (4.5–12 meters) long. It was a powerful swimmer, moving through the water by flapping its wide, paddlelike flippers. Some species had very long necks and small heads equipped with sharp teeth. They may have darted their heads at moving prey. Other species had shorter necks and long heads.

Size: Top: part of a backbone, 4 in (10 cm) across; Bottom: ribcage and backbone of a different animal, section shown about 53 in (135 cm) long
Distribution: Worldwide
Time range: Lower Jurassic

Ichthyosaurus

This was a streamlined sea-living reptile. The specimen shown here is part of the animal's flipper. Whole skeletons have been found —one such fossil of *Ichthyosaurus* also showed the outline of the body. These fossils indicate that *Ichthyosaurus* was similar in form to present-day dolphins. Some fossil skeletons of adult ichthyosaurs carried the skeletons of young inside. It seems that, like dolphins, *Ichthyosaurus* gave birth to live young.

Size: Adults grew to about 10 ft (3 m) long
Distribution: Worldwide
Time range: Triassic to Cretaceous

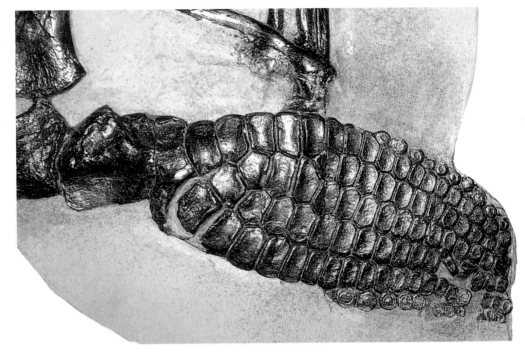

Temnospondyl

This is the earliest known complete skeleton of an amphibian. It was found in Scotland. If you look at the photo carefully, you can see that the specimen's hind legs had five toes and the front legs had four. This specimen was found in limestone rocks. Other fossils found in the same rock layer included spiders, scorpions, and other amphibians, which indicates that *Temnospondyl* was living on land, not in water.

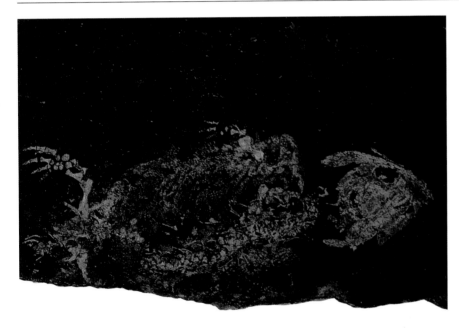

Size: This specimen is 16 in (40 cm) long
Distribution: United Kingdom, North America, and Australia—Time range: Lower Carboniferous

What About Dinosaurs?

Dinosaurs ruled the earth for about 160 million years. They came in many shapes and sizes. Most of what we know about the dinosaurs comes from studying fossils of their bones.

Two different groups

Dinosaurs are divided into two major groups according to the way their hip bones were arranged. **Saurischians** (pronounced: *saw-RISH-ee-ans*) were the "lizard-hipped" dinosaurs. Their lower hip bones fan out where the leg joins the hip, like the hip bones of lizards. The **ornithischians** (pronounced: *OAR-nee-THISH-ee-ans*) were the "bird-hipped" dinosaurs. Their lower hip bones sweep backward.

Dinosaur fossils

Dinosaur fossils have excited scientists for nearly 200 hundred years. Many complete dinosaur skeletons have been found.

Tyrannosaurus rex skull

For other species, we have only a bone or two. The shape and arrangement of the bones can tell us a lot about how dinosaurs lived. Nearly half the known skeletons have been unearthed since the 1940s, so our knowledge has grown tremendously in recent years. Fossilized nests of dinosaur eggs and of baby dinosaurs suggest to us how dinosaur mothers looked after their young. A recent exciting discovery was a *Tyrannosaurus* thigh bone that still contained some bone marrow.

Tyrannosaurus was a saurischian dinosaur.

Stegosaurus was an ornithischian dinosaur.

Make models of dinosaurs

These simple models will show you how two kinds of dinosaurs stood and how their weight was balanced. **You will need**: modeling clay, pencils, a clothespin, used matchsticks, and scissors.

Two-legged meat-eaters, like *Tyrannosaurus,* are known as theropods. *Tyrannosaurus* had a body that was fairly short. Its huge head had strong jaws packed with razor-sharp teeth, while the long tail balanced the weight of the head.

1 **Mold the clay** into the shape of the *Tyrannosaurus*'s body.
2 **Use a clothespin** to represent the heavy jaw.
3 **Use pencils** for the two strong back legs.
4 **Use matchsticks** that were already burned by an adult for the small front limbs.
5 **The long pencil tail balances** the weight of the head at the hips.

Make a dinosaur wall chart

You can make a dinosaur wall chart decorated with postcards or pictures from magazines and newspapers. Stick them on to a large sheet of poster board. You might divide the chart into "bird-hipped" and "lizard-hipped" dinosaurs, or into meat-eaters and plant-eaters. Your chart could also feature a prehistoric time line. Use a piece of poster board that is wider than it is high. Divide it into the different geological periods. Then paste or glue your pictures of fossils and dinosaurs under the section showing the period in which they lived.

Four-legged plant-eaters, like *Diplodocus*, are known as sauropods. Sauropods walked on four legs and had a long neck and tail. Many of the truly huge dinosaurs—such as *Seismosaurus* and *Apatosaurus*—were sauropods. *Diplodocus*, which grew to about 90 feet (27 meters) in length, was a fairly large sauropod. It used its tail to counterbalance its long neck.

1. **Mold the clay** into the shape of the *Diplodocus*'s body.
2. **Use four pencils as legs**. See how they have to be placed differently from those of the *Tyrannosaurus* to make the model stand up.
3. **Use a long pencil for the neck,** and another for the tail.
4. **Make a small head** with a lump of clay.

Tyrannosaurus

Diplodocus

Find Out More

Glossary

amber: hard, yellowish-brown fossilized resin that comes chiefly from pine trees that lived millions of years ago; it sometimes contains preserved remains of insects and other organisms

ammonite: extinct mollusk with a spiral-shaped shell

arthropod: any of a large group of animals with jointed legs, such as insects, spiders, and lobsters

calcium carbonate: limestone

carapace: shell or bony covering on the back of some animals, such as lobsters and turtles

coprolite: fossilized excrement

core: name for the center of the earth; the core is made mostly of molten iron

crust: outer layer of the earth

erosion: wearing away of rocks by the action of wind or water

evolution: theory describing the process by which plants, animals, or other organisms change over time

exoskeleton: hard outer case or shell of some invertebrates

fossil: remains or markings of a once-living plant or animal found within rock

invertebrate: animal without an internal backbone

magma: molten (melted) rock beneath the earth's surface

mantle: layer of very hot rock under the earth's crust and on which the plates carrying the continents and ocean floor float

mollusk: soft-bodied animal without a backbone; most mollusks, such as snails and clams, have shells

ornithischian: "bird-hipped" dinosaur with lower hipbones that swept backwards, like those of a bird

petrification: type of fossilization in which a dead organism's body is slowly replaced with minerals

plate, continental: section of crust and upper mantle that moves about, carrying a continent

resin: sticky yellow or brown substance that flows from certain trees and other plants

saurischian: "lizard-hipped" dinosaur with lower hipbones that fanned out where the leg joins the hips

sedimentary rock: rock made from layer upon layer of mud, sand, and plant and animal remains, which have been compressed together deep underground, often under the sea

sediments: tiny pieces of rock, weathered by wind or water, which make up sedimentary rock

species: particular type of organism

strata: layers of sediment, compressed together into sedimentary rock

trace fossil: fossil that shows tracks, trails, burrows, or other signs of an ancient animal, rather than the remains of its body

trilobite: type of extinct sea-dwelling arthropod

vertebrate: animal with an internal backbone

zone fossil: fossil of a particular species that is used for estimating the age of rocks

Organizations

The **American Federation of Mineralogical Societies** is a hobby- and education-oriented group dedicated to the study and appreciation of earth sciences, including fossil hunting. It publishes the *A.F.M.S. Newsletter.* Contact: American Federation of Mineralogical Societies, 2706 Lascassas Pike, Murfreesboro, Tennessee 37130-1540; (615) 893-8270. http://www.amfed.org

The **American Paleontological Society** is at the forefront of organizations promoting fossil hunting and paleontology. http://www.paleosoc.org

In Canada, the **Geological Survey of Canada** is the best source for information about fossils. Contact: the Geological Survey of Canada, Natural Resources Canada, Earth Sciences Sector, 601 Booth St., Ottawa, Ontario K1A 0E8; (613) 996-3919. http://www.nrcan.gc.ca/gsc/index_e.html

The **U.S. Geological Survey** is one of the best sources of information about fossils and fossil-bearing deposits in the United States. For information, contact: Earth Science Information Center, 12201 Sunrise Valley Drive, Reston, Virginia 20192; (888) 275-8747. http://www.usgs.gov

Index

Additional Resources

Audubon Society Field Guide to North American Fossils Ida Thompson (Knopf, 1982).

Collecting Fossils Steve and Jane Parker (Sterling Publications, 1997).

Fossils Cyril Walker and David Ward (Dorling Kindersley, 2002).

Outside and Inside Dinosaurs Sandra Markle (Atheneum, 2000).

Index

hyena, 73

I

Icthyosaurus, 75
Iguanodon, 74
Illaenus, 57
inner core, of the earth, 6
Inoceramus, 36
insect, in amber, 9
interambulacra, 24
invertebrate, 4, 18–65
Isastraea, 23

K

Ketophyllum, 22
kingdom, 4
Kosmoceras, 44

L

lava, 6
Lepidodendron, 13
Leptaena, 60
Leptolepis, 71
Libellula, 59
limestone, shelly, 8
limpet, 47, 50
Lingula, 60
Lithostrotion, 22
lobster, 59
Lonsdaleia, 23
Lopha, 34
lungfish, 66, 72
Lytoceras, 43

M

macroconch, 44
Macrocrinus, 28
magma, 7
mammal, 4, 66, 72, 73
Mammuthus, 73
Mantelliceras, 45
mantle
  of mollusk, 32
  of the earth, 6
map, geological, 16
Mariopteris, 13
Merycoidodon, 72
Mesolimulus, 58
Metopaster, 28
microconch, 44

mineral, 8
Modiolus, 36
mollusk, 32–51
Monograptus, 65
Mourlonia, 47
Myophorella, 35

N

Natica, 50
nautiloid, 40
Nautilus, 40
Neuropteris, 14
Nuculana, 32

O

Odontaspis, 72
Ogyginus, 54
Ogygiocarella, 56
Ogygiocaris, 56
Ogygopsis, 54
Olenellus, 54
Oreodon, 72
organism, 4
ornithischian, 76
Orthoceras, 40–41
ossicle, 28
outer core, of the earth, 6
oxygen, from plants, 10
Oxytoma, 33
oyster, 34, 37

P

Palaeocoma, 29
Pangaea, 6
Paradoxides, 55
Parkinsonia, 45
Parmulechinus, 27
Pecopteris, 13
pedicle, 60
pedicle valve, 60
Pentacrinites, 29
Permian Period, 18
Peronopsis, 55
petrification, 8
Phacops, 56
Pholadomya, 37
photosynthesis, 10
phyla, 4
Phyllograptus, 65
pinnule, 28

Plagistoma, 35
Planorbis, 50
plant, 4, 10–15
Platysomus, 70
Plectothyris, 63
Plesiosaurus, 74
Pleuroceras, 42
Pleurotomaria, 49
Poleumita, 47
polyp, 21
Productus, 62
projects
  dinosaur, 38, 76–77
  housing fossil collection, 52–53
  looking for fossils, 16–17
  origin of fossils, 30–31
  trace fossils, 38–39
prokaryote, 4, 15
Prolecanites, 41
Promicroceras, 42
protist, 4
Pseudopecten, 37
Psiloceras, 9, 43
Pterygotus, 58
Ptychodus, 72
Pustula, 61
pygidium, 54
Pygope, 63

Q

Quenstedtoceras, 44

R

reptile, 4, 66, 74–76
rhabdosome, 64
Rimella, 49
rock
  dating of, 9
  fossil formation in, 8
  movements in the earth, 6–7
  see also sedimentary rock; strata

S

sand dollar, 25
Satapliasaurus, 38
saurischian, 76
sauropod, 77

scaphopod, 4, 46
Schizodus, 32
Schizophoria, 60
scientific names, 2
Scolicia, 39
Scyphocrinites, 29
sea lily, 28–29
sea urchin, 24–27
sediment, 5, 6
sedimentary rock, 5–9, 16
seed fern, 12–14
Seismosaurus, 77
septa, 21
shark, 72, 73
shell
  arthropod, 54
  brachiopod, 60
  mollusk, 32, 40
  sea urchin, 24
shelly limestone, 8
Silurian Period, 66
siphon, 32
siphonal notch, 47
Siphonia, 20
siphuncle, 40
slipper limpet, 50
slug, 47
snail, 47
Solenopora, 15
species, 4
Sphenopteris, 12
spicule, 20
Spirifer, 61
Spondylus, 36
sponge, 20
squid, 40
starfish, 28–29
Stegosaurus, 76
stipe, 64
Straparollus, 47
strata, 5, 30
stromatolite, 15
Sycostoma, 49
syncline, 30

T

tabulae, 21
tectonic plate, 6, 7
teeth, fossil, 72–73
teleost, 69
Temnospondyl, 75

Index

See *World Book's Science & Nature Guides Resources & Cumulative Index* volume for a chart showing the geological time periods.